CW00554784

OCR GCSE

Economics

www.heinemann.co.uk

✓ Free online support
✓ Useful weblinks
✓ 24 hour online ordering

0845 630 44 44

Christopher Bancroft
Amy Chapman
Clive Riches

OCR
RECOGNISING ACHIEVEMENT

Heinemann

Official Publisher Partnership

OCR AND HEINEMANN WORKING TOGETHER TO PROVIDE BETTER SUPPORT FOR YOU

Heinemann is an imprint of Pearson Education Limited, a company incorporated in England and Wales, having its registered office at Edinburgh Gate, Harlow, Essex, CM20 2JE. Registered company number: 872828

www.heinemann.co.uk

Heinemann is a registered trademark of Pearson Education Limited

Text © Christopher Bancroft, Amy Chapman and Clive Riches

First published 2009

13 12 11 10
10 9 8 7 6 5 4 3

British Library Cataloguing in Publication Data
A catalogue record for this book is available from the British Library.

ISBN 978 0 435 84905 4

Designed by Tek-Art, Crawley Down, West Sussex, UK
Typeset by Tek-Art, Crawley Down, West Sussex, UK
Illustrated by Tek-Art, Crawley Down, West Sussex, UK
Cover photo/illustration © Getty Images/Frederic Cirou
Printed in Malaysia (CTP-VP)

The websites used in this book were correct and up-to-date at the time of publication. It is essential for tutors to preview each website before using it in class so as to ensure that the URL is still accurate, relevant and appropriate. We suggest that tutors bookmark useful websites and consider enabling students to access them through the school/college intranet.

Acknowledgements
The authors and publisher would like to thank the following individuals and organisations for permission to reproduce photographs (t = top, b = bottom, l = left, r = right):

Alamy/Charles Polidano/Touch the Skies p. 39; Alamy/David Pearson p. 16; Alamy/Jochen Tack p. 118; Corbis pp. 3, 20, 129r; Corbis/EPA/Aaron Ufumeli p. 65; Corbis/Eye Ubiquitous/Sean Aiden p. 42; Corbis/Moodboard p. 125l; Corbis/Reuters/Arko Datta p. 125r; Digital Stock p. 41; Digital Vision pp. 4b, 56, 129; Ford Motor Company p. 96; Getty Images/AFP/Mike Simmonds p. 105; Getty Images/Daniel Berehulak p. 76; Getty Images/Hulton Archive p. 60; Getty Images/Jeff J Mitchell p. 61; Getty Images/PhotoDisc pp. 6 (table), 9l, 19, 23bl, 23r, 27r, 33, 51, 67, 69, 70l, 70r, 78, 93, 95; Getty Images/Popperfoto/Bob Thomas p. 13; Getty Images/Steve Eason p. 133; Getty Images/Taxi p. 85; Getty Images/Tim Graham Photolibrary p. 71; Getty Images Sport/Alex Livesey p. 27l; Image Source Ltd pp. 108, 111t; Naki Photography p. 129l; PA Images/AP/Scott Heppell p. 97b; Pearson Education Ltd/Ann Cromack, Ikat Design p. 3; Pearson Education Ltd/Arnos Design p. 9r; Pearson Education Ltd/Debbie Rowe pp. 111b, 124; Pearson Education Ltd/Gareth Boden p. 38; Pearson Education Ltd/Jules Selmes pp. 25, 32, 97t; Pearson Education Ltd/Mind Studio p. 66; Pearson Education Ltd/Naki Photography p. 102; Pearson Education Ltd/Rob Judges p. 68; Pearson Education Ltd/Studio 8, Clark Wiseman pp. 6, 23tl; Shutterstock/Gytis Mikulicius p. 1; Shutterstock/Monkey Business Images p. 4t; Stockbyte p. 40

Every effort has been made to contact copyright holders of material reproduced in this book. Any omissions will be rectified in subsequent printings if notice is given to the publishers.

Chris Bancroft has taught in a Leicestershire comprehensive school for many years as Head of the Economics and Business Studies department. He is Chief Examiner for OCR GCSE Economics as well as an examiner for AS level Economics. His previous publications include *Assignments in Economics* (1989).

Amy Chapman was a member of the specification development team for OCR GCSE Economics and is Principal Examiner for the unit 'The UK economy and globalisation'. She has been a Principal Examiner for GCSE Economics since 2004. Amy is Head of Economics and Business Studies at Cheltenham College.

Clive Riches is an education consultant, having previously been Head of Economics and Business in both state and independent schools and a Director of Commercial Activities. He has extensive experience of examining at both A and GCSE levels, including being a Chief and Principal examiner. He is author of numerous articles and a co-author of *Core Economics*, and is responsible for material on GCSE Economics on the EBEA's website.

Contents

Get ready for GCSE Economics

This GCSE is designed to inspire you and encourage an interest in real-world economics.

Once you have followed this course and performed well, you can legitimately call yourself an **economist**.

How is the GCSE course structured?

Your OCR GCSE is made up of **three** units, which are externally assessed – you are set an exam for each unit. There is no assessed coursework.

This book is divided into three parts to match the three units.

What exams do I have to take?

Each unit has an exam. The format of the exam papers is shown below.

Unit A591: *How the Market Works*	
25% of the total GCSE marks. 1 hour computer-based test. 60 marks.	This question paper consists of **12** questions:
	You are required to answer **three** sets of questions; each set of questions is based on a particular theme or case study and will include some short-answer and some data interpretation questions, as well as some extended prose. Each set of questions is worth 20 marks.

Unit A592: *How the Economy Works*	
25% of the total GCSE marks. 1 hour written paper. 60 marks.	This question paper consists of **three** semi-structured questions:
	You are required to answer **three** semi-structured questions; each question is based on a particular theme or case study and will include some short-answer and some data interpretation questions, as well as some extended prose. Each question is worth 20 marks.

Unit A593: *The UK Economy and Globalisation*	
50% of the total GCSE marks. 1 hour 30 minutes written paper. 80 marks.	You are required to answer questions based on pre-released stimulus material. Some questions may involve data interpretation. (The raw mark for A593 is 80. However, because it is given a 50% weighting, this is converted to a mark out of 120 for the grade threshold table shown on page vi.)

All three papers have compulsory questions – there is no choice between questions. This is fairer because everyone answers the same questions, and you do not have to waste time reading questions that you will not answer.

Papers 1 and 2

Paper 1 is based on the content of Unit 1, and paper 2 is based on the content of Unit 2. The main difference between them is that paper 1 is taken at a computer: the questions are on the screen and you key in your answers. Each paper will have quite a wide coverage of content.

Paper 3

Paper 3 is the longest, at 1.5 hours, and is the most important – it counts for 50% of the grade. It is based on a **pre-released case study**, which is issued to you many weeks before the exam and gives you time to become familiar with the case on which the questions will be based. You do not know what the questions are before the exam itself, but you will be able to identify the topic areas on which the questions will be set. You are likely to be given work based on the case study to do in class, and this will make you more confident on the day of the exam.

But note: although paper 3 is based mainly on the content in part 3 of this book, it may require knowledge and understanding of content found in parts 1 and 2 also.

Specimen papers

OCR has produced specimen exam papers and mark schemes, which are available on its website (www.ocr.org.uk). The actual papers that you take will be in a very similar format to these.

What are the assessment objectives?

These are the skills which you should be able to demonstrate on your GCSE course, and which will be assessed in the exam.

Ao1 Demonstration of knowledge and understanding

You should be able to recall, select and communicate your knowledge and understanding of concepts, issues and terminology.

Ao2 Application of knowledge and understanding

You should be able to apply skills, knowledge and understanding in a variety of contexts.

Ao3 Analysis and evaluation of evidence

You should be able to analyse and evaluate evidence, make reasoned judgements, and present appropriate conclusions.

You will be assessed in all three skills on all three papers. These are in equal proportions on paper 3. On papers 1 and 2, objectives 1 and 2 are each worth a slightly larger percentage of the marks than objective 3.

What is the relationship between assessment objectives and exam questions?

The questions on the exam papers have **command words** and phrases. These tell you what you are required to do, and give you a clue about which assessment objectives are being tested.

Here are a few examples to show you what this means.

Q. **Name** two taxes collected by the UK government.

Q. **State** two taxes.

You only have to demonstrate **knowledge**.

In these cases you do not even have to write a sentence. If you answered 'income tax and value added tax', for example, you would receive full marks.

Q. **Explain what is meant by** unemployment.

In this case you have to write in sentences. You are being asked to demonstrate your **knowledge and understanding** of an economic term by explaining it.

Q. Some data are given about a textile factory closing in a town. **Explain the effects** of the closure of the factory on the local area.

In this case some **application** is required. You are not simply being asked about the effects of factories closing. You are being asked about the effects of the closure of a particular factory in a specific area. You are applying your knowledge and understanding to the particular case. Note that the pre-released case study gives plenty of scope for application.

Q. **Explain how** a change in the rate of interest may help to control the future rate of inflation.

There is **analysis** required here. You are required to explain how a change in one economic variable (interest rate) will affect another variable (inflation).

Q. **Discuss** the effects on the economy of a high rate of inflation.

Q. **Should** the government put a high rate of tax on cigarettes? **Give reasons** for your answer.

In both these cases there is **evaluation** required for full marks. (You can still get some marks without evaluating because not all the marks for these questions would be for evaluation.) This means you should consider all sides of an issue and reach an overall judgement (conclusion), which you justify.

When do I take my exams?

This will depend on the policy that your school or college operates. This course provides the opportunity to take exams in the first year of a two-year course. You could take the Unit A591 exam in June of year 10, and A592 and A593 at the end of the course; or A592 in year 10 and A591 and A593 at the end.

You may be able to take both A591 and A592 in the first year. Retakes are allowed, so you could also retake A591 and/or A592 at the end of the course if you needed to.

How do my exam marks translate into grades?

There are a total of 240 marks for the three papers, and the marks are converted into grades as shown in the table below.

	Grade							
Maximum uniform mark	A*	A	B	C	D	E	F	G
240	216	192	168	144	120	96	72	48

How can I do well in my exams?

- First, you need to be familiar with the content of the course. The more confident you are about the terms, concepts, issues and theories found on the course, the better you will perform.

- Second, remember that knowledge and understanding is not being tested alone. In the exam room you are also expected to demonstrate your ability to apply, analyse and evaluate. If you have practised writing answers to exam-type questions during the course, you are more likely to perform well in the exam room. There are sample exam-type questions following each part of this book (pages 50, 92 and 140).

- Third, the pre-released case study provides a great opportunity to do well. You know that the questions on the paper for Unit 3 will be based on this case study.

- Finally, each of the three parts of this book concludes with an **Exam Café** section (pages 44, 86 and 134). These provide advice and guidance on doing well in the exams – so read them carefully!

General introduction

Economics is a subject that is about you – what you spend, how you live and what affects your life. It covers your local area, your country and the whole world. It is about things that affect you now and in the future. It is a live and vibrant subject.

This book will enable you to gain an understanding of how the economy works and how economists look at the economy. From the very beginning you will be able to test your understanding of economics by applying your learning to what is happening around you, both locally and nationally.

The aim of this book is to:

- introduce you to what economics is about
- allow you to look at the world around you from an economic perspective
- enable you to have a greater understanding of issues in the news
- provide opportunities to apply your understanding of economics
- introduce websites and other resources where you can extend your knowledge and understanding
- help you to be successful in your exams through revision sections at the end of each unit.

The book, like the exam, is divided into three units. These start with what you are likely to have some familiarity with, then move outward to firms and the whole economy, and finally to the issues of international economy.

Unit 1 is titled 'How the market works'. This covers issues that directly affect consumers and workers:

- the basic economic problem
- how markets work, including demand and supply and price determination
- how firms operate in markets, including wages.

Unit 2 is titled 'How the economy works'. This looks at economics in terms of the national economy:

- key economic objectives – economic growth; inflation and unemployment
- government revenue and expenditure, including taxation
- government policies – fiscal, monetary and supply-side.

Unit 3 is titled 'The UK economy and globalisation'. This places the UK economy within the context of the world economy:

- trade, including globalisation, free trade versus protection and the European Union
- UK trade
- international competitiveness, including exchange rates
- the position of less-developed countries and world poverty.

Each chapter is clearly linked to an identified area of the specification. This will allow you to monitor what you have done, and how much more has to be covered. You will know also that if a topic is not in the book, it is not going to be tested in your exams. Don't forget, however, that as economics is going on around you, things change, so you must keep up to date and this is expected by the examiners.

Within each chapter, not only will you learn about new concepts, ideas and theories to do with economics, but you will be provided with the key terms you are expected to know, and you will often have opportunities to revisit areas already covered to reinforce your understanding. In addition, you will be able to develop the skills needed to use your knowledge successfully – both in your exams, and also in terms of current news stories and in your own life.

Each chapter is based on the following features, although not all may appear every time:

- brief introduction – setting the scene for you
- 'learning outcomes' – which match those in the specification
- 'activities' and 'apply it'– a chance for you to show your understanding
- 'for debate' – opportunities to develop the skill of discussion
- 'taking it further' – a chance to develop greater knowledge and understanding.

These should all help to make learning about economics more fun, as well as increasing your chances of doing well in the exams.

At the end of each unit there are sections designed to help you prepare for the exam. These are called 'exam cafe' and 'exam preparation'. Not only are there tips on how to revise and how to improve your chances in the exam, but there is a checklist to help you make sure you have fully covered all aspects of the units and are confident about them. In addition, there are questions and answers from students, with examiners' comments to show you why some answers get high marks while others are less successful, and how these could be improved.

Economics can seem difficult at first. There is a new 'language' to learn of terms and diagrams. There is a new way of thinking. Remember, you have already been doing subjects such as mathematics for eight years, whereas economics as a subject is new to you. Remember that you can contribute from your own experiences – you have already been involved in many economic activities, such as demanding goods and services, having to decide what to spend your money on, or travelling to another country. Make good use of the activities in the book to get yourself into the subject – and do use economics on a daily basis. The more economics you do, and the more you use it, you will realise how helpful it is to you in understanding the world in which you live.

Now read on and enjoy your first taste of economics.

Part 1 How the market works

What is a market? It is any place where buyers and sellers meet, where goods and services are bought and sold. The buyers and sellers often have physical contact with each other – for example, when you go into a shop to buy a snack, or when you pay your fare on a bus. But this is not necessarily the case – for example, when the internet is used, or in the case of the stock market. In this part of the book we will find out how markets work.

Think of all the things you have spent money on during the past week. Perhaps some snack food and drink, a visit to the cinema, an item of clothing, a birthday present for your friend. Think of the things your household spent money on, like electricity, gas and water supply, food and petrol. Everything you and your household bought had a price. How was this price determined?

Fresh air is one of the most important things for all of our lives. We need it to breathe in order to live. Yet we don't have to pay for it; it is what economists call a free good. How is it that people don't pay for something so vital, and yet are willing to pay a very high price for something fairly useless, such as diamonds? The answer to this lies in the concept of scarcity. Resources are scarce when there are not enough to satisfy human wants. What we mean by resources, and the implications of scarcity, are considered early in this part of the book.

As resources are scarce, they have to be allocated somehow. This is the function of markets – to allocate resources. Consumers demand goods and services, and firms supply them. If consumers demand more of a particular product, then its price will tend to rise. This shows the firms that producing it has become more profitable, and they will be willing to supply more. Meanwhile, firms will produce less of the products for which demand has fallen, as this has become less profitable. We will find out more about demand, supply, price and profits in this part of the book.

Firms will need land, capital and labour to produce the output, and these also have markets. You are likely to be part of the labour market when you have finished your education, and perhaps earlier if you have a part-time job. The price of labour is the wage, so we will also consider how this is determined and why some jobs are much better paid than others. Perhaps the study of economics will help you to become one of the better-paid workers or to become an entrepreneur (page 5) with your own firm.

1 What is the economic problem?

1.1 Defining the economic problem

What is the study of economics all about? The central purpose of economic activity is to combine resources in order to produce output that will meet our **needs** and **wants**. You will learn that **resources** are scarce, and wants are infinite. So we have a problem – the basic economic problem.

LEARNING OUTCOME:

The next two pages will help you to:

- identify and understand examples of the four factors of production
- understand what is meant by the basic economic problem.

Needs, wants and resources

Our needs and wants are very different. We need some things just to stay alive – including water, food and warmth. But our wants are never-ending (infinite). We may want a Nintendo Wii™ for Christmas. Do we actually need it to stay alive? Most people would say no – it is simply a luxury that would be nice to have. Imagine you get a Wii for Christmas – what will you want for your birthday? An iPod®, perhaps. The cycle of wants continues, once you get one thing, you move straight on to wanting another.

KEY TERMS

Needs – something essential to survival – food, water, warmth, clothing and shelter.

Wants – something you would like to have, but is not essential to survival – for example cars, mobile phones and chocolate.

Resources – something used to produce output.

In contrast, the resources used to produce these goods and services are in limited supply (finite). Collectively, resources are called factors of production. Resources can be divided into four groups (right).

1 Labour

Labour is the human input into the production process. Not all labour is of the same quality. Every person has different skills and qualifications – we call this human capital.

When people have more human capital, they are likely to be more productive. This means they can produce more in the same period of time.

LABOUR

LAND ← Factors of production: the resources we have available to produce goods and services → CAPITAL

ENTERPRISE

Mirza is a baker. He has been working as a baker for two weeks. He has been making 50 cakes a day since he started. We can therefore say his **productivity** is 50 cakes per day. Mirza's boss decides that he needs to do some more training, so asks him to take an NVQ in cookery. After taking this qualification, Mirza is able to make 60 cakes a day. His productivity has increased. His human capital has also increased.

State ten resources Mirza might use to make his cakes. Put each resource under one of the following four headings:

- labour
- capital
- land
- enterprise.

KEY TERM

Productivity – output per worker per period of time.

AO1 and AO2 skills ACTIVITIES

- How does your human capital differ from your teacher's? Using two columns, list the elements of your human capital and your teacher's human capital.
- Is there a difference between the human capital of a cleaner and that of a doctor?

2 Land

Land includes both the land itself and all the natural resources on and below the land, which are available for production. Although this resource is named 'land', it also includes water resources such as the sea, rivers and lakes, and the resources (such as fish) within them. Some countries have a large amount of a particular natural resource and are able to specialise in the extraction and production of it, for example oil drilling in Saudi Arabia and gold mining in South Africa.

It is not necessarily true that a country with a large area of land has more resources than a smaller country. The quality of the land is very important, including the resources that lie within it. A large desert country with few known mineral reserves may not be as productive as a small country with a temperate climate that is very suitable for agriculture.

3 Capital

Capital refers to goods that are used to produce other goods and services. Examples of capital include factories, machinery, plant and equipment. Spending on capital is known as investment. Examples of capital used to provide the service of education in your school include the classrooms, desks, computers, textbooks, science labs, catering equipment, telephones, and so on.

4 Enterprise

Enterprise is having ideas and taking risks in setting up or running a business. An entrepreneur is someone involved in taking those risks, perhaps by putting in their money, or having the ideas and the drive to set up or run the business.

FOR DEBATE

Which of these people take risks that might be thought of as 'enterprise' in a business?

- Customers
- Staff
- Shareholders (owners)
- Management

The reward for being an entrepreneur is profit.

A well known example of an entrepreneur is Richard Branson. As a young man, he took a risk by opening a record store named Virgin. Now he heads a large multi-product company which runs airlines, trains, financial services, soft drinks, mobile phone services and other services. Rock and pop singers and authors can be considered to be entrepreneurs who invest in their own talents. Thus individuals such as Madonna or J K Rowling have made large profits from putting their ideas into practice.

LEARNING TIP

Some students find it hard to remember the four factors of production. Try remembering the word CELL – each letter stands for one of the factors of production. Capital, Enterprise, Land, Labour.

AO1 and AO2 skills ACTIVITIES

Mr Tino owns a sweet-making factory. His factory employs 50 people and uses machinery to produce the sweets.

Describe how each of the four factors of production might be used in the production of sweets.

1.2 Scarcity, choice and opportunity cost

The main purpose of economic activity is to produce goods and services to satisfy consumers' needs and wants. This means that firms produce to satisfy people's need for consumption, both as a means of survival, and also to meet their growing demands for an improved lifestyle or standard of living.

LEARNING OUTCOME:

The next two pages will help you to:

- understand what is meant by the basic economic problem
- understand why and how choices are made
- apply the concept of opportunity cost to all economic decision-makers
- show appreciation of how resources are allocated by individuals, firms and governments
- understand the meaning of the primary, secondary and tertiary sectors.

Production of goods and services

Goods are items that you can touch (tangible) – you can take them home and use them. An example of a good is a pen or a packet of crisps.

A service is something that someone provides for you; you cannot touch it (intangible). Examples include tourism and banking.

 **ACTIVITIES**

- State four goods that you have bought this week.
- State two services that you have bought this week.

Sector	Description	Examples
Primary	Where the extraction of raw materials takes place	Mining, farming, fishing, oil extraction, forestry, quarrying
Secondary	Where raw materials are manufactured into goods	Car manufacturing, furniture manufacturing, manufacture of electronic goods, for example computers, mobile phones
Tertiary	The service sector	Banking, tourism, education, public transport, entertainment, health services, insurance, advertising

The production of nearly all goods and services uses up scarce resources.

Production takes place in one of three sectors, as shown in the table (left).

The basic economic problem

The basic economic problem occurs because resources are scarce – but our wants are infinite.

As resources are scarce and our wants are never-ending, we have to allocate resources. When we allocate resources, we ask the following questions.

- What goods and services should we produce?
- How should the economy use its resources to operate schools or hospitals?
- What mix of goods will it produce?
- What is the best way to produce goods and services?
- What is the best use of scarce resources?
- Who is to receive goods and services?

How resources are allocated

In a market economy, resources are allocated through the free working of the market (price) mechanism of demand and supply. In a nutshell, consumers decide what they want to buy, and producers (firms) use resources in order to supply it. In a mixed economy, such as the UK, this is also the case; but in addition the government will allocate resources to providing particular services, such as education and healthcare.

In this part of the book we will consider in more detail how resources are allocated, particularly in units 1.3, 2.8 and 2.9.

Opportunity costs and choices

We already know that resources are scarce and we have infinite wants. This creates a problem; if we cannot have everything we want, we have to make choices. I really want to go on holiday and I would like a new car. I do not have the money to do both, so I must decide which I would like to do the most. If I choose to go on holiday, it means I cannot buy a new car. I can therefore say that the **opportunity cost** of going on holiday is buying a car. This means that when I have chosen the holiday, the next best alternative is the car.

1.3 Approaches to the economic problem

We now know that resources are scarce and wants are infinite. We must therefore allocate resources carefully. In this section we will learn how different economies allocate resources in different ways.

KEY TERMS

Market – where buyers and sellers meet to exchange goods and services. This does not have to mean a face-to-face meeting.

Market economy – where all resources are allocated by private individuals and groups.

Planned economy – where all resources are allocated by the government.

Mixed economy – where some resources are allocated by the government, and other resources are allocated by private individuals and groups.

Market and mixed economies

A **market economy** is an economy where all resources are allocated by the forces of demand and supply, basically by buyers and sellers, with a price attached. All resources are privately owned, and people act in their own self-interest. In a free-market economy, there is no government involvement in the allocation of resources.

At the other extreme, in a **planned economy** all resources are allocated by the government. The government owns everything and controls prices and incomes.

A **mixed economy** is somewhere in between free-market and planned economies. The government owns and allocates some resources, and the free market (buyers and sellers) own and allocate others.

A01, A02 and A03 skills ACTIVITIES

- In pairs, think of three advantages of a free-market economy.
- In pairs, think of three advantages of a planned economy.
- The UK economy is a mixed economy. Why do you think this is a good way to allocate resources fairly?

Public and private enterprises

The UK economy is a mixed economy – this means that some resources are allocated by the government and some are allocated by buyers and sellers.

This means we have some organisations owned and run by the government, while other firms are owned and run by private individuals.

 **ACTIVITIES**

- List **three** businesses/organisations owned by the government.
- List **three** businesses/organisations owned by private individuals or groups of people.

The public sector

The public sector includes organisations owned and run by the government, such as hospitals and schools, which are not there to make a profit. The government runs these organisations in order to make sure these vital services are provided. These services provide benefits not only to those using them, but also to people who are not directly involved (positive externality).

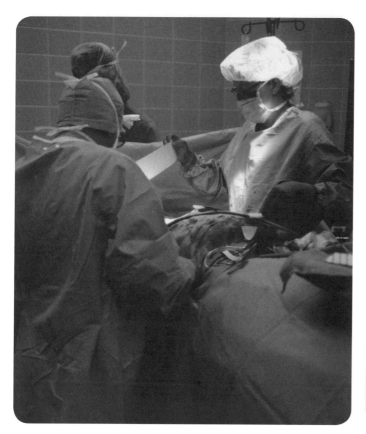

Paul works for the NHS as a human resources manager. His wife, Janet works for a small, family-run shop in the village where they live.

Which person works in the private sector, and which person works in the public sector?

- Explain what is meant by the term 'public sector'.
- Who runs and funds the private sector?

In the UK economy, the government accounts for approximately 40% of economic activity.

- List **three** benefits you will gain through going to school and achieving five good GCSEs.
- List **two** benefits that other people, such as your neighbours, will gain from your going to school and getting five good GCSEs.

The private sector

The private sector includes organisations owned and run by private individuals or groups. Their main objective is to make the largest possible profit. They will also have other objectives, such as to increase in size, to have a greater market share, or to provide a high-quality product or service. In bad times, such as recession, the main objective of many firms may be to survive.

KEY TERMS

Public sector – the government sector of the economy, where organisations are owned and run by the government.

Private sector – the sector of the economy where firms are owned and run by private individuals and groups – their main aim is profit maximisation.

Should healthcare in the UK be provided by the public or private sector?

1.4 What is specialisation?

We all specialise in something – perhaps without realising it. We do things that we are good at and enjoy doing. In this section we are going to discover why people, firms and countries specialise.

LEARNING OUTCOME:

The next two pages will help you to:

- understand the meaning of specialisation
- explain how and why individuals, firms and countries specialise
- explain and evaluate the costs and benefits of individuals/firms specialising
- appreciate the use of money as a medium of exchange, a unit of account, store of value and means of deferred payment.

Specialisation can occur on a number of levels. As individuals, we specialise in what we are best at, for example you have chosen a smaller number of subjects to study to GCSE; I have specialised as an Economics teacher. Firms specialise, for example Virgin Atlantic provides flights. Regions specialise, for example Sheffield specialised in steel. And countries also specialise, for example the UK specialises in financial services.

Why do we specialise?

We specialise in something we are skilled at and will become better at, and so we will be able to produce more of that good or service. If I had to produce all my own food and clothing, and therefore be self-sufficient, I could only produce what I needed. I would never really become skilled at producing one item, because my tasks would be changing all the time. If I specialised in making one item, I would become better at it (more productive) and therefore I could produce more. What could I do with the extra that I produce and don't need (**surplus**)? I could exchange it with someone else for something they have produced. This specialisation means that we can satisfy our needs and wants more easily.

Labour: a numerical example

Rahi and Jameel each make and sell toys. Rahi makes 50 toys in 10 hours but takes 30 hours to sell them. Jameel, on then other hand, takes 30 hours to make 50 toys but only 10 hours to sell them. With no specialisation, they each make and sell 50 toys in 40 hours, therefore 100 toys are made and sold in 80 hours of work.

If they specialise in their areas of expertise (Rahi makes toys and Jameel sells them), then total output increases greatly. In 40 hours, Rahi can make 200 toys, while Jameel can sell 200 toys in 40 hours, so now 200 toys are made and sold in 80 hours of work – a 100% rise in output.

Land: a numerical example

Field X when divided into two halves can grow 100 tonnes of wheat but only 20 tonnes of rice. Field Y when divided into two halves can grow 100 tonnes of rice but only 20 tonnes of wheat. The total output from the two fields is 120 tonnes of wheat and 120 tonnes of rice.

If we introduce specialisation, field X can produce 200 tonnes of wheat and field Y can produce 200 tonnes of rice. There are now an extra 80 tonnes of each product brought about through specialisation.

This example is realistic if we consider that the two fields are located in different parts of the world. Field X has the climate and soils suitable for wheat, field Y for rice.

KEY TERM

Surplus – when more is produced than is required. The surplus can be exchanged for money or other goods/services.

The costs and benefits of specialisation

Specialisation will create benefits for both the firm and the workers. The following table shows potential benefits to both the firm and the workers.

Benefits to the firm	Benefits to the workers
Workers become quicker at producing goods (more productive)	Specialised workers tend to get higher pay
Because of increased productivity, production becomes cheaper per good (lower average costs)	Workers' specific skills will be improved
Production levels are increased	More motivation from job satisfaction

But there are also costs of specialisation, to both the firm and the worker, as shown in the table below.

Costs to the firm	Costs to the worker
Greater cost of training workers	Boredom for the worker as they do the same job every day
Quality may suffer if workers become bored by the lack of variety in their job	Workers' skills may suffer as they are only doing one job
More expensive workers	Workers may eventually be replaced by machinery

For specialisation to work well, there has to be an efficient means of exchange.

FOR DEBATE

- In pairs, write down three benefits to Virgin Atlantic of specialising in transatlantic flights.
- In pairs, write down three costs to myself of specialising as an Economics teacher.

Money

So far in this section we have talked about exchanging goods and services. But in the modern world, most people sell goods and services for money. Money plays an important role in all our lives. When we talk about money, we are not talking just about notes and coins. We are also talking about money in bank accounts.

The functions of money

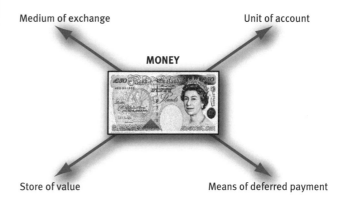

Medium of exchange   Unit of account

MONEY

Store of value   Means of deferred payment

Medium of exchange

When we go into a shop to buy a magazine, we must hand over some money – we say we are exchanging our money for the magazine. Money is used as a medium of exchange – this is probably the most common use of money.

Unit of account

If I were to say that a magazine is £1, I am giving this magazine a monetary value (unit of account). This function of money is also known as a measure of value.

Store of value

If I put £100 in the bank today, when I go back to the bank in a month's time I will be able to take my £100 out again – it has kept its value (store of value).

Means of deferred payment

We can also take out loans or agree future payments, perhaps if we do not have the money straight away. We can agree a figure to pay and a time period over which payments should be made, deferring the payment by borrowing the money (means of deferred payment). We will consider money in more detail in unit 6.2.

 **ACTIVITIES**

State and explain two reasons why people might save money.

FOR DEBATE

If the supply of money were to increase significantly, what would happen to the value of money?

2 What are competitive markets?

2.1 Markets

If you have many options – if there are many suppliers of what you want – you can shop around and make an informed choice to get the best value you can. And if the suppliers know what other sellers in the market are offering, they can compare goods and prices, and offer better deals to attract your custom. This is a **competitive market**.

LEARNING OUTCOME:

The next two pages will help you to:

- explain what is meant by a competitive market
- understand the implications of operating in competitive markets.

KEY TERM

Competitive market – a market situation in which there are a large number of buyers (demand) and sellers (supply).

Being in a competitive market means that:

- there are a large number of firms in the market
- new firms can set up easily in the market
- firms know what their competitors are doing.

How do firms compete?

It is generally accepted that a high level of competition is needed for a market to work well. Developments in information technology, particularly with the internet, mean that many markets have moved towards a more competitive situation. Buyers are able to know more about products, and can shop around. Firms are able to compare prices and specifications more easily. When a market is not competitive, we say that the market is failing.

The following explanation is from the government's Department for Business, Enterprise & Regulatory Reform.

'Competitive markets provide the best means of ensuring that the economy's resources are put to their best use by encouraging enterprise and efficiency, and widening choice. Where markets work well, they provide strong incentives for good performance – encouraging firms to improve productivity, to reduce prices and to innovate; whilst rewarding consumers with lower prices, higher quality, and wider choice. By encouraging efficiency, competition in the domestic market – whether between domestic firms alone or between those and overseas firms – also contributes to our international competitiveness.'

(Source: www.berr.gov.uk/whatwedo/businesslaw/competition/index.html)

The implications of competitive markets

Implications for consumers

There are strong benefits for consumers from competitive markets, as referred to in the quote above. Consumers can 'shop around' to get the highest quality and/or the lowest prices. They are faced with variety and choice. Firms will try hard to innovate in order to provide new products that benefit consumers, whether they are new features for mobile phones, new drugs for particular diseases, or a new topping for a pizza crust. In retailing, firms will compete through location, opening hours and providing good customer service.

There may be some disadvantages of competition, for example, if all the firms are small they cannot gain economies of scale (see unit 3.4) and cannot pass on the benefits of low average costs in lower prices. Some consumers may become confused by a

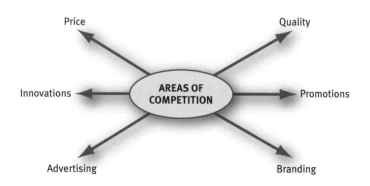

lot of competition. Overall, however, there are great benefits of competition to consumers. In this age of the internet, consumer knowledge (about what is available, where and at which prices) is greater than ever.

Implications for firms

A firm that can successfully supply the goods or services consumers want, at a price they wish to pay, will thrive and earn profits for itself. It may be able to grow larger and gain market share. On the other hand, firms that fail to satisfy consumers sufficiently will eventually fail. This applies as much to a huge multinational firm such as General Motors as to a small business such as a café in the local community.

If you were to walk along Blackpool promenade you would find a large number of shops selling sticks of rock. You could get your name put in the middle, or that of your favourite football team. The rock may be peppermint flavour, or strawberry. Whatever type of rock you choose, they are all essentially the same. There are many sellers along the promenade, all offering similar products. There are also many buyers – hundreds of thousands of people walk along the promenade each year and buy rock to take back to their friends and family.

- Explain what is meant by a competitive market.
- To what extent does competition benefit the holidaymakers in Blackpool buying rock?
- To what extent does competition benefit the sellers of rock in Blackpool?

- Give **one** real-world example of each way in which firms can compete.
- Explain **two** reasons why competition is good for consumers.
- Why does competition drive a business to become more efficient?

When a market is not competitive, that usually means it is not working well (failing), which is often unfair to the consumer. In an uncompetitive market, a small number of firms hold all the power.

Somerfield (4%)

Other (21%)

Tesco (31%)

Asda (17%)

Sainsbury's (16%)

Morrisons (11%)

- To what extent do supermarkets operate in a competitive market?
- Identify five examples of ways in which supermarkets compete with each other.
- Do consumers benefit from competitive markets? Give reasons for your answer.

TAKING IT FURTHER

- Make a list of four supermarkets close to where you live. How do these supermarkets try to persuade you and your parents to buy goods and services from them?
- Think about how they encourage you to enter the store, what they do inside to persuade you to buy, and any extras they offer.

2.2 Monopoly and monopoly power

In the previous section we talked about competitive markets, where there are many buyers and sellers. We now turn our attention to a market where there is just one seller, or where there is one very dominant firm. We are going to look at both the benefits and the costs of **monopoly**, and how the government can ensure that a firm with **monopoly power** acts in the public's best interests.

> ### LEARNING OUTCOME:
>
> The next two pages will help you to:
> - explain the meaning of monopoly power
> - describe and evaluate the causes and consequences of monopoly power
> - explain and evaluate the role of government in promoting competition.

When a market is not competitive, we can say that it is not working well and is unfair to the consumer. An uncompetitive market will have a small number of firms holding all the power. When firms have this monopoly power, there is an inefficient allocation of resources by the price mechanism (forces of demand and supply).

> **KEY TERM**
> **Monopoly** – a situation where there is only one firm selling in a market. For example, before 2006 Royal Mail was a monopoly, being the only firm to provide the service of letter delivery.

How do firms achieve monopoly power?

There are a number of ways in which a firm can achieve monopoly power.

- **Merger and takeover** – when two firms come together to form one, consumers no longer have as much choice because there are fewer firms in the market. The newly merged firm can take advantage of this by raising prices and lowering the quality of the product.

- **Statutory monopoly** – this occurs when key industries are given monopoly status by the government. An example of this is water companies – if you live in Nottingham, the only company that can provide you with tap water is Severn Trent. The government created regional monopolies with the water industry, as it would be too difficult to have a number of firms providing water to the same area.

- **Internal expansion** – if a firm builds more factories or more shops, it will be able to generate more sales and therefore in the long run increase its market share.

- **Branding** – when buying ketchup or baked beans, how many of you would always buy Heinz? Even if they increased the price? I only buy Heinz tomato ketchup and Heinz baked beans – I am drawn in by the branding and am a loyal customer. So if the price changes, I am still inclined to stay with Heinz. Heinz has created monopoly power through branding.

- **Cost barriers** – large firms may gain internal economies of scale, which means their average costs are low. This enables them to keep prices below the price at which small firms could enter the market. As no new competition enters the market, the existing firm retains its monopoly power.

> **KEY TERM**
> **Monopoly power** – when a firm has more than 25% of the market share. Tesco has a legal monopoly in the supermarket industry, it holds approximately 31% of the market share (see unit 2.1). This means that 31% of all supermarket sales happen at Tesco.

Evaluating the consequences of monopoly

When we talk about monopolies, we tend to talk about how bad they are for us as consumers. But monopolies can be a good thing, too.

Why a monopoly can be bad

- **High prices** – due to lack of competition, a firm with monopoly power can charge higher prices because the consumers have no choice. If we think in terms of demand for a good provided by a monopoly, we can say that demand is very inelastic (if the price increases, demand will fall by only a small proportion). Here demand is not very responsive to changes in price, because there are no alternatives for consumers to choose, so they must buy the product at the price offered to them. Price elasticity of demand is considered in more detail in unit 2.5.

- **Poor quality** – due to lack of competition, the firm has no incentive to improve the quality of its product or service.

Why a monopoly can be good

- **Research and development** – a monopoly enjoys high profit levels, which it can put back into the firm to research and develop new products and methods of production, which will benefit the consumer in the long run.

- **International competitiveness** – a large firm with monopoly power in the UK is able to build up advantages that will help it in international markets and therefore it will be more competitive abroad. An example is Corus, the UK/Dutch steel company.

- **Exploitation of economies of scale** – as a firm grows larger, it is able to benefit from its large size and so average costs fall. If average costs fall, the firm can choose either to reduce prices or to make a bigger profit. We will discuss economies of scale in more depth later (see unit 3.4). Not all firms with a monopoly power choose to raise their prices, for example Tesco and Toys R Us market themselves as inexpensive stores.

ACTIVITIES

AO1, AO2 and AO3 skills

You are an investigative journalist who has been asked to write a report about how the UK Government promotes competition. Find out about what the Competition Commission does (www.competition-commission.org.uk) and produce a short newspaper article.

Evaluating monopoly – a summary

When evaluating, we need to consider the details of each situation. Is the firm a pure monopoly with 100% of the market, or one with some degree of monopoly power? If it has some monopoly power, how strong is it? For example, Tesco has 31% of UK supermarket sales, so does this mean that its customers suffer from high prices and a lack of choice? Most would argue that there is enough competition, so Tesco's customers benefit. However, if Tesco has the only supermarket in a particular town, then perhaps this is bad for consumers and possibly prices are higher than in Tesco stores elsewhere.

We should also consider consequences for the firm itself. We would usually expect a monopoly position to be good for the firm and allow it to earn high profits. But it is possible that in the long run a firm may become complacent and fail to keep up with changes in consumer tastes or changes in technology. For example, the Post Office has lost customers to email.

We may also wish to consider effects on others in the community, as well as the customers and the firm. The firm may exploit its workers with low pay if there is no alternative employment in that industry. The huge retailer Walmart in the USA is often accused of this. On the other hand, a firm in a secure monopoly position may not be too concerned about keeping its costs down, and may pay its workers generously. For example, driving a London Underground train is not a particularly skilled job but it pays very well.

A large firm with monopoly power can also have consequences for smaller competitors and potential competitors. Tesco, for example, has been accused of 'land grabbing', which involves buying up land that is a possible site for a supermarket to prevent rivals from opening a store there. Monopolies may also have periods of predatory pricing, reducing prices to a level where competitors are unable to compete and are forced to leave the market, and then raising prices again. Nevertheless, small firms can and do compete against firms with some degree of monopoly power. Pizza Hut and Domino's, for example, are large firms that benefit from economies of scale, but small pizza outlets also survive in the local community, offering customers benefits such as convenient location and opening hours.

2.3 Demand

What you want to buy – and what you are able to buy (which may well not be the same thing!) – at a particular time will be affected by a number of different factors. These are the factors that affect **demand**. Here we are going to look at demand – what it is, and what can cause it to change.

LEARNING OUTCOME:

The next two pages will help you to:

- explain what is meant by demand
- construct an individual demand curve and a market demand curve from consumer data
- explain movements along the demand curve.

FOR DEBATE

Collect five adverts for goods or services you or members of your family would buy. Also, find out the price of each product. In groups, discuss whether the price would make you want to buy the product.

- Is it a fair price?
- Does the advert make you want to buy the product?
- Is there anything else that would make you want to buy the good or service?

 **ACTIVITIES**

AO2 skills

Task 1

You must decide how many cans of coke (or other fizzy drink in a can) you will buy in one week when the price is at a particular level. In the table, fill in the number of cans next to the price.

Price	Number of cans
10 p	
20 p	
30 p	
40 p	
50 p	
60 p	
70 p	
80 p	
90 p	
£1	

Now put your results into a graph. Put the number of cans on the *x* axis and the price on the *y* axis. Join the dots together to make a line graph.

- What is the shape of the line?
- Can you explain this?
- How does your line differ from the person's next to you? Do they start in different places? Is one steeper than another?

Task 2

As a class, add up your demand for a can of fizzy drink at each price level. Draw the demand curve for the class.

ACTIVITIES

Identify three situations in which your demand is not effective.

Demand and price

For virtually all products, consumers buy more when the price decreases and less when the price increases. The relationship between price and quantity is inverse.

The diagram shows the demand curve for Mars Bars in a school.

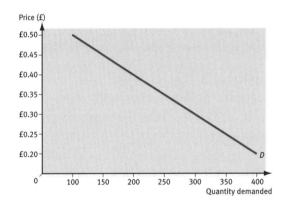

Movements along the demand curve

Movements along the demand curve are caused by a change in the price of the good itself. This is either a contraction or an extension of demand.

If the price of a good falls, individuals who already buy it will be able to afford more of it. This explains why, for an individual's demand curve (such as your demand for Mars Bars), the quantity demanded rises with a fall in price. This is also true for a market demand curve (such as the school population's demand for Mars Bars). In addition, the quantity demanded will rise as price falls in the market because new consumers will enter that market to buy the good at a lower price.

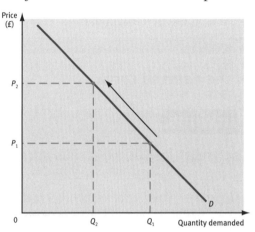
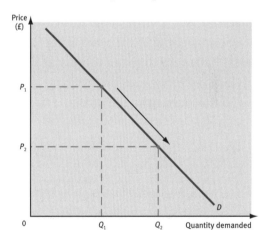
LEARNING TIP

It is really important that when you draw a demand curve you label it, and label the axes. If you forget your labels you will lose marks in the exam.

2.4 The demand curve – rise or fall?

We have considered what demand is, and how a change in price will affect movement along the demand curve. We will now go on to discuss other factors that cause demand to rise or fall.

Shifts in the demand curve

As discussed on pages 16–17, a change in the price of the good itself causes a movement along the demand curve. We are now going to turn our attention to other factors that cause demand to increase or decrease. These factors cause the demand curve to shift either to the right or to the left.

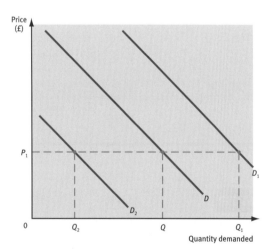

As you can see on the diagram, if the demand curve shifts to the *right*, demand has *increased*. If demand shifts to the *left*, demand *decreases*.

Factors that cause the demand curve to shift

You have already discussed in pairs what you think might increase or decrease demand for a good or service. How many of the following did you get?

• **P**opulation
• **A**dvertising
• **S**ubstitutes (price of)
• **I**ncome
• **F**ashion and trends
• **I**nterest rates
• **C**omplements (price of)

Population

An increase in the population will cause an increase in demand. This will cause the demand curve to shift to the right.

Advertising

Consider the market demand for Nike trainers. If Nike decides to increase the advertising budget by £5 million, people will become more aware of Nike trainers and therefore more likely to buy them. Demand for Nike trainers will increase and the demand curve will shift to the right.

Substitutes (price of)

Substitute goods are goods that can be used instead of each other. An example is Pepsi and Coca Cola. If the price of Coca Cola fell, the demand for Pepsi would fall, because people would change from Pepsi to Coke. This would cause the demand curve for Pepsi to shift to the left.

Income
If average income falls (for example in a recession), the demand for normal goods will fall and the demand curve will shift to the left.

> **KEY TERM**
>
> **Inferior goods** – goods for which the demand falls when income rises. An example may be bus journeys. As people's incomes rise, they can afford to buy their own vehicles and the demand for bus journeys falls.

Interest rates
Interest rates are the extra a person pays the bank when borrowing money, and the reward for saving. If interest rates rise, it will be more expensive for people to borrow money. So if you are buying a big ticket item, for example a holiday or a car, which may require a loan, demand is likely to fall, which will cause the demand curve to shift to the left.

Complements
Complementary goods are goods that are in joint demand – if you buy one, you will need to buy the other. One example is a DVD player and DVDs. If the price of DVDs falls, the demand for DVD players is likely to rise.

ACTIVITIES

Activity 1
How will the demand curve for a normal good shift in each of the following cases? Circle the answer you think is correct. You have five minutes for this task.

a) The price of a substitute good falls.

  left   right   no shift

b) Population rises.

  left   right   no shift

c) Tastes shift away from the good.

  left   right   no shift

d) The price of a complementary good falls.

  left   right   no shift

e) The good becomes more expensive.

  Left   right   no shift

Activity 2
Consider the demand curve for petrol. What effect will the following have? Tick the answer you think is correct.

a) An increase in the price of cars.

left shift	right shift	contraction	extension
☐	☐	☐	☐

b) An increase in the proportion of the population owning cars.

left shift	right shift	contraction	extension
☐	☐	☐	☐

c) A rise in the transport costs of shipping oil.

left shift	right shift	contraction	extension
☐	☐	☐	☐

d) A growing concern for environmental issues by the general public.

left shift	right shift	contraction	extension
☐	☐	☐	☐

e) An increase in duty on diesel.

left shift	right shift	contraction	extension
☐	☐	☐	☐

f) A reduction in tax on petrol.

left shift	right shift	contraction	extension
☐	☐	☐	☐

For each of the situations above, draw a fully labelled diagram showing the change to demand.

2.5 Price elasticity of demand

So far we have considered what demand is (pages 16–17) and what will cause it to increase or fall (pages 18–19). We will now look at the gradient of the curve and see how responsive demand is to changes in price.

Along with price elasticity of supply, price elasticity of demand (PED) is one of the harder concepts to learn and understand at GCSE.

What does PED measure?

PED measures the responsiveness of the quantity demanded to a change in the price of a good.

This means that we look at how much the price has changed by, and what this has done to quantity demand – has it increased by a large percentage, or by a small percentage?

In order to work out the PED of a good or a service, we use the following formula:

$$PED = \frac{\text{percentage change in quantity demanded}}{\text{percentage change in price}}$$

Let us assume that a firm reduces the price of its product by 10% and quantity demanded rises by 20%. Using the formula for PED, we get

+20% / –10% = –2.

Technically, PED is always a negative figure because price and quantity move in opposite directions. However, we often ignore the minus sign when explaining the meaning of elastic and inelastic demand, as in the table opposite. Returning to the example here, a value of 2 means that the quantity demanded changes at twice the rate of the price change.

Suppose another firm also reduces the price of its product by 10% but quantity demanded only rises by 5%. In this case the value of PED is

+5% / –10% = –0.5.

A value of 0.5 means that the quantity demanded changes at half the rate of the price change.

The first firm had an *elastic* demand for its product with a numerical value greater than 1 (ignoring the minus sign), while the second firm had an *inelastic* demand for its product with a numerical value less than 1 (ignoring the minus sign). The different types of PED are summarised opposite.

AO1 and AO2 skills **ACTIVITIES**

In pairs, consider the demand for petrol. What is likely to happen to the demand for petrol if the price goes up? Why will this happen? Can you show this using a demand curve?

Consider the demand for a luxury holiday to the Caribbean. What is likely to happen to demand for a £1000 holiday if the price drops by £200? Why will this happen? Can you show this on a demand curve?

Can you see any differences in the two demand curves you have drawn? What are they?

What does it all mean?

Type of PED		Numerical value (ignoring the minus sign)	Description
Perfectly inelastic demand		0	The quantity demanded remains the same although the price changes, i.e. demand is **completely unresponsive** to a change in price
Inelastic demand		< 1	The quantity demanded changes at a **lesser rate** than price
Unit elastic demand		1	The quantity demanded changes at the **same rate** as the price
Elastic demand		> 1	The quantity demanded changes at a **greater rate** than price
Perfectly elastic demand		Infinity	Any quantity is demanded at a **given price**

Why is PED important for a firm?

So a firm knows the PED for its product – what does it do with this information? The PED is very important for firms when they are making pricing decisions. It helps them decide what to do with price if they want to increase **total revenue**.

KEY TERM

Total revenue – the amount of money a firm receives when selling its product. (At this stage we do not consider total costs.)

total revenue = price × quantity sold

Most firms want to increase their total revenue. So they need to decide what they must do to price in order to achieve this.

If the demand for a product is elastic (demand is very responsive to changes in price), the firm must *decrease* its price in order to *increase* total revenue.

If the demand for a product is inelastic (demand is not very responsive to a change in price), the firm must *increase* its price in order to *increase* total revenue.

FOR DEBATE

Why is PED always negative?

PED and total revenue: a worked example

Assume a firm sets the price of its product at £10 per unit, and its sales are 2000 units a week.

The firm's total revenue is:

£10 × 2000 = £20 000 per week.

Assume the firm now raises the price of its product to £11 per unit, and its sales fall to 1900 units a week.

The firm's total revenue is:

£11 × 1900 = £20 900 per week.

We know that the demand for the product is price inelastic (a numerical value of less than 1) because a rise in the price has led to a rise in total revenue.

It is possible to calculate the value of the PED from the information above.

$$\text{Percentage change in quantity demanded} = \frac{\text{change in quantity}}{\text{original quantity}} \times 100$$

$$= \frac{-100}{2000} \times 100 \qquad = -5\%$$

$$\text{Percentage change in price} = \frac{\text{change in price}}{\text{original price}} \times 100$$

$$= \frac{1}{10} \times 100 \qquad = 10\%$$

Therefore

$$\text{PED} = \frac{\text{percentage change in quantity demanded}}{\text{percentage change in price}}$$

$$= \frac{-5}{10} \qquad = -0.5$$

ACTIVITIES

In each of the following cases, calculate:

- the original total revenue
- the new total revenue
- the value of PED.

a) Original price £10   Original sales 500
   New price £9   New sales 600

b) Original price £5   Original sales 1000
   New price £6   New sales 800

c) Original price £2.00   Original sales 8000
   New price £2.50   New sales 7000

d) Original price £200   Original sales 40
   New price £180   New sales 50

AO1 and AO2 skills ACTIVITIES

- Draw a demand curve showing the demand for a product that is **inelastic**. Show on your diagram an increase in price. Now shade in the two areas of total revenue. Has total revenue increased?

- Now do the same, but this time with an **elastic** demand curve.

Factors that influence PED

Number of close substitutes within the market
The more (and closer) substitutes are available in the market, the more elastic demand will be in response to a change in price.

Luxuries and necessities
Necessities tend to have a more inelastic demand curve, whereas luxury goods and services tend to be more elastic. For example, the demand for opera tickets is more elastic, as it is seen as a luxury.

Percentage of income spent on a good
It may be that the smaller the proportion of income spent that is taken up with purchasing the good or service, the more inelastic demand will be.

Habit-forming goods
Goods such as cigarettes and drugs tend to be inelastic in demand.

Time period under consideration
Demand tends to be more elastic in the long run rather than in the short run.

AO1 and AO2 skills **ACTIVITIES**

- A firm knows that the PED for its product is **−0.7.**
  a) What does this figure mean?
  b) Draw a diagram to show the elasticity of the demand curve.
  c) What should the firm do with the price of its product in order to increase total revenue?
- A firm knows that the PED for its product is **−1.5.**
  a) What does this figure mean?
  b) Draw a diagram to show the elasticity of the demand curve.
  c) What should the firm do with the price of its product in order to increase total revenue?

2.6 Supply

So far we have only talked about one half of the market – demand. We will now go on to look at the part producers play in the market, and how they make decisions on what and how much to **supply**.

LEARNING OUTCOME:

The next two pages will help you to:
- explain what is meant by supply
- construct an individual firm's supply curve and a market supply curve from production data
- explain shifts of, and movements along, the supply curve.

KEY TERM

Supply – the quantity a producer is willing and able to produce at a given price in a given period.

 **ACTIVITIES**

- Using the data below, construct a supply curve. The axes are the same as for the demand curve (page 17) – price on the *y* axis and quantity on the *x* axis.

Price (£)	Quantity
10	500
20	600
30	700
40	800
50	900

- What do you notice about this line?
- What is the relationship between price and quantity?
- Why do you think this relationship exists?

The supply curve

The supply curve you have constructed in the above activity could be that of an individual firm. It is willing to supply more at a higher price. A market supply curve will be of a similar shape, and is constructed from the sum of the supply from all the firms in that market. More suppliers will enter the market when the price rises, because supplying the product is now more profitable.

Movements along the supply curve

As with the demand curve (see page 17), a movement along the supply curve is caused only by a change in **price** of that good.

 **ACTIVITIES**

- Draw two diagrams – one to show an **extension** in supply, and one to show a **contraction** in supply. Make sure you label both diagrams fully.
- If you are unsure, remember:
  - the supply curve is upward-sloping
  - *contraction* means a *reduction* in supply and *extension* means an *increase* in supply.

Shifts in the supply curve

A shift in the supply curve works in very much the same way as for the demand curve (page 18). The main difference is in the slope of the curve.

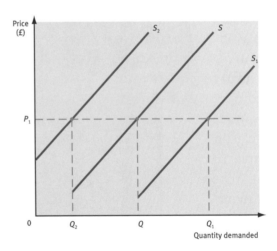

The diagram shows that:
- when the supply curve shifts to the right, there is an increase in supply
- when the supply curve shifts to the left, there is a decrease in supply.

What causes the supply curve to shift?

- **P**roductivity – if the productivity (output per worker per period of time) of a firm increases, it can increase the quantity supplied and therefore shift the supply curve to the right.

LEARNING TIP

It is really important that you learn the seven factors that cause the supply curve to shift. The mnemonic **PINTSWC** may help – can you come up with a sentence using those initial letters that you will easily remember?

- **I**ndirect taxes – when the government increases a tax on a good such as petrol, the supply shifts to the left. We will look at indirect taxes in more detail on pages 66–69.

- **N**umber of firms entering the market – if more firms enter the market to supply a particular good, then overall supply will increase and supply will shift to the right.

- **T**echnology – if a firm uses better, more advanced technology in the production process, it is likely to produce more in the same period of time. This will cause supply to increase and the supply curve to shift to the right.

- **S**ubsidies – if the government gives a firm a subsidy, then supply will shift to the right. We will discuss this in more detail on page 31.

- **W**eather – if the growth of a crop is affected by poor weather, the harvest may be less than in previous years, thus reducing the supply – the supply curve shifts to the left.

- **C**osts of production – if the costs associated with producing a good or a service, such as wages, raw materials and rent, go up, then a firm will reduce the amount it supplies as it is less likely to make a big profit. This will cause the supply curve to shift to the left.

AO1 and AO2 skills ACTIVITIES

- How will the supply curve for a normal good shift in each of the following cases? Circle the answer you think is correct.

  a) The cost of production of a good falls.

  left   right   no shift

  b) The government gives a firm a subsidy.

  left   right   no shift

  c) A firm increases its productivity.

  left   right   no shift

  d) The government puts an indirect tax on the good.

  left   right   no shift

  e) The firm uses improved technology to produce the good.

  left   right   no shift

- Consider the supply curve for petrol. What effect will the following have?

  a) An increase in the price of petrol.

  left shift   right shift   no shift   contraction   extension

  b) The government gives Shell a subsidy to try to be more environmentally friendly.

  left shift   right shift   no shift   contraction   extension

  c) Shell has developed new technology to extract oil to produce petrol.

  left shift   right shift   no shift   contraction   extension

  d) The number of firms selling petrol increases.

  left shift   right shift   no shift   contraction   extension

- Choose two of the above situations, and for each case draw a fully labelled diagram to show what has happened to the supply of petrol.

2.7 Price elasticity of supply

We have considered what causes supply to increase and decrease (pages 24–25). Now we will look at the gradient of the supply curve and discuss how responsive supply is to a change in price – the price elasticity of supply (PES).

LEARNING OUTCOME:

The next two pages will help you to:

- understand the meaning of price elasticity of supply
- understand and construct graphs to illustrate price elasticity of supply
- understand the implications of price elasticity of supply.

AO1 and AO2 skills ACTIVITIES

- Using the information in the table, have a go at drawing a supply curve to show each of the five different types of elasticity of supply. You must draw five separate diagrams.
- Which type of elasticity is likely to be that of the supply of tickets for an FA Cup Final, or the supply of tickets for a sought-after concert? Why do you think this?

What does PES measure?

PES measures the responsiveness of quantity supplied to a change in price.

In order to work out the PES, we use the following formula:

$$PES = \frac{\text{percentage change in quantity supplied}}{\text{percentage change in price}}$$

FOR DEBATE

Why is PES always positive?

Factors that influence PES

Level of spare capacity

If a firm is not using all of its resources in the production of the good or service, we say that it is working below its full capacity. If price were to suddenly increase and the firm had spare capacity, it would be able to react very quickly and increase supply. Therefore when there is spare capacity, supply is very responsive to a change in price.

What does it all mean?

Type of PES	Numerical value	Description
Perfectly inelastic supply	0	The quantity supplied remains the same as the price changes, i.e. supply is **completely unresponsive** to a change in price
Inelastic supply	< 1	The quantity supplied changes at a **lesser rate** than price
Unit elastic supply	1	The quantity supplied changes at the **same rate** as the price
Elastic supply	> 1	The quantity supplied changes at a **greater rate** than price
Perfectly elastic supply	Infinity	Any quantity is supplied at a **given price**

Production lags

If we take the agricultural market, such as the market for wheat, the time between planting the seeds and harvesting the wheat is a number of months, therefore the supplier of wheat cannot easily respond to changes in the price due to the time lag involved.

Substitutability of factors of production

If a firm can easily move the factors of production it uses in producing its goods between production lines, then it will be more able to respond quickly to changes in the price. Supply will be more elastic in this case.

Time period

In the short run, supply will be fairly inelastic. This is because a firm can't change its production process quickly. But in the long run, supply will be fairly elastic, because a firm can alter its scale of production over time.

APPLY IT!

The City Ground is where Nottingham Forest play their home matches. The capacity of the City Ground is 30 576.

- How can we describe the supply of seats at the City Ground (hint – using PES)?
- Draw a supply diagram to show the supply of seats at the City Ground.
- Using your diagram, draw a demand curve that shows an equilibrium price of £30. Make sure you label your diagram clearly.
- If Nottingham Forest decide to set a price of £20 per match, what effect will this have on the market for Nottingham Forest tickets?

Level of stocks and work in progress

If a firm has a low stock level, it will not be able to respond quickly to changes in price. In this situation, supply would be fairly inelastic.

 **ACTIVITIES**

AO1 and AO2 skills

- A firm knows that the PES for its product is **0.2**.
    a) What does this figure mean?
    b) Draw a diagram to show the elasticity of the supply curve.
- A firm knows that the PES for its product is **1.6**.
    a) What does this figure mean?
    b) Draw a diagram to show the elasticity of the supply curve.

2.8 Determination of price in competitive markets (1)

So far we have discussed demand and supply separately. Markets occur when buyers and sellers meet and exchange goods and services. We must now put together demand and supply to see how changes in these affect both price and quantity.

Market mechanism

When buyers (demand) and sellers (supply) meet to exchange goods and services, we have a market, as shown in the diagram below.

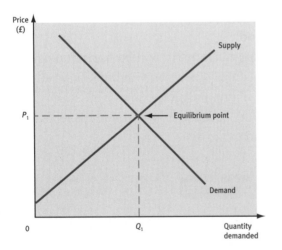

On this diagram, the point where demand and supply meet is called the **equilibrium**. We also say that the equilibrium is where the market clears – because this is the price at which supply equals demand. This point is important because at the equilibrium price, buyers are able to buy exactly the quantity they want and producers are able to sell exactly the quantity they wish to sell.

KEY TERM
Equilibrium – the point where demand and supply meet.

The equilibrium will change only if one of the factors that determines demand or supply changes and leads to a shift in one of the curves. For example, the diagram below shows what happens when demand rises, so the demand curve shifts to the right.

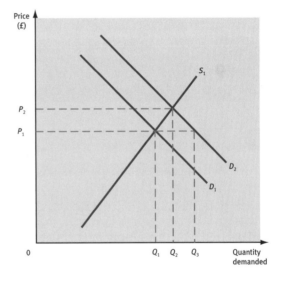

Once demand has risen, P_1 is no longer the equilibrium price. In fact, at price P_1 there is now disequilibrium as Q_1 is supplied but Q_3 is demanded. The price will automatically rise in the market until a new equilibrium is reached. We can see that this is at price P_2 where quantity Q_2 is both demanded and supplied. Thus a rise in demand has led to a rise in price and an increase in the quantity bought and sold.

The following diagram illustrates what happens when supply rises, so the supply curve shifts to the right.

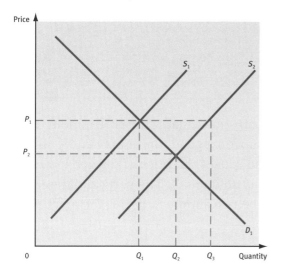

The original equilibrium price is P_1 where demand equals supply. When supply rises to S_2 there is now disequilibrium at price P_1 because Q_1 is still demanded but Q_3 is supplied. The price will automatically fall in the market until a new equilibrium is reached. We can see that this is at price P_2 where quantity Q_2 is both demanded and supplied. Thus a rise in supply has led to a fall in price and an increase in the quantity bought and sold.

Price in competitive markets

A competitive market occurs when there is no single individual firm that can influence the price. In a competitive market, the price is determined by the forces of demand and supply.

AO1 skills
ACTIVITIES

• Draw a diagram to illustrate a fall in demand. Explain how this will affect the price and sales of the product.
• Draw a diagram to illustrate a fall in supply. Explain how this will affect the price and sales of the product.

APPLY IT!

State the effect of each situation on the market – whether it will affect the supply or demand curve, and whether it is a contraction, extension, a shift right or a shift left.

Market	Situation
The Times	Rise in the price of *The Times*
Fish	The UK government gives fishermen a subsidy to help reduce their costs
Ford Focus	Rise in the price of a Toyota Avensis
Bus travel	Rise in real incomes
The Times	Fall in the price of *The Guardian*
CDs	Fall in the cost of producing CDs
Levi's® jeans	Successful TV advert
Cigarettes	The government increases the tax on cigarettes by 5p a packet

Pick four of the markets/situations listed, and for each one draw the demand curve (one market must be a contraction, one an expansion, one a shift to the left and the last a shift to the right). Write a couple of sentences explaining what is happening.

TAKING IT FURTHER

With the aid of a demand and supply diagram, explain:

• the factors that have caused the increase in ownership of mobile phones in the UK
• how Coca Cola spending £60 million on extra advertising will affect the price and quantity of Coca Cola sold
• how the cost of syrup increasing (used to make Pepsi) and a trend towards drinking fizzy mineral water will affect the price and quantity of Pepsi sold.

2.9 Determination of price in competitive markets (2)

When discussing supply, we briefly covered indirect taxes and subsidies as factors that cause the supply curve to shift (pages 24–25). Here we consider in more detail what indirect taxes and subsidies are, and their effect on price and quantity sold. We also look at minimum and maximum prices.

LEARNING OUTCOME:

The next two pages will help you to:
- explain the effects of taxes and subsidies on price and quantity in competitive markets
- explain the effects of maximum and minimum prices.

Indirect taxes

Indirect taxes are taxes on spending. Instead of going directly to the government from our income, indirect taxes are paid by the retailer/producer of the good or service we buy. There are two types of indirect tax: specific and *ad valorem*.

> **KEY TERM**
> **Specific tax** – a tax placed on a good or service which is a specific amount of money per unit bought, for example £2 tax on each bottle of wine.

An example of a specific tax is excise duty. It shifts the supply curve to the left, parallel to the original supply curve as in the following diagram.

The diagram shows that if the government increases a specific tax on a good, the supply curve shifts to the left and causes the price of the good to rise and the quantity sold to fall. The vertical difference between the two supply curves is the amount of tax per unit.

TAKING IT FURTHER

- Does the price increase caused by the increase in indirect tax match the amount of tax placed on the good?
- If the consumer does not pay all of the tax, who pays the other part?
- Draw two diagrams side-by-side. One should have an elastic demand curve, the other should have an inelastic demand curve. How does the elasticity affect the amount the consumer pays in tax? Do you think this is fair?

> **KEY TERM**
> *Ad valorem* **tax** – a tax placed on a good or a service which is a percentage of the price.

An example of an *ad valorem* tax is VAT (see pages 67–69). This type of tax shifts the supply curve to the left and is steeper in gradient than the original supply curve, as in the diagram below.

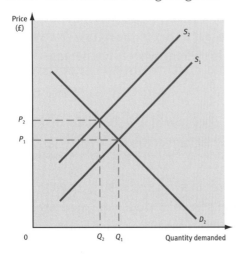

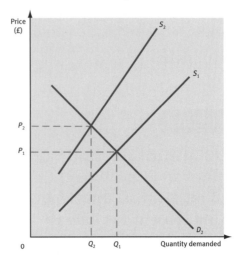

Subsidies

A subsidy is a payment given to a firm, usually by the government. It may be for one or more of the following reasons – to:

- lower price
- increase supply
- encourage locating in an area of high unemployment
- help firms produce in a more environmentally friendly way
- help firms become more efficient.

A subsidy will cause supply to rise so the supply curve will shift to the right. Price will fall and the quantity will rise.

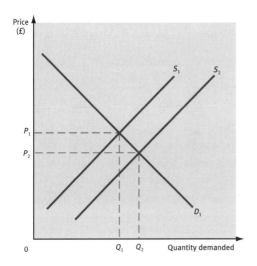

FOR DEBATE

Do you think that giving a firm a subsidy is the best method of improving its efficiency? List reasons for your answer, and discuss them in class.

Minimum and maximum prices

In some markets, the government believes that the price is unfair, so they intervene in that market by imposing a maximum or minimum price.

Minimum price

A minimum price is set above the equilibrium, and the price is not allowed to go below it. As you can see on the following diagram, this can cause excess supply. At the minimum price of P_{min}, Q_2 will be demanded but Q_3 will be supplied.

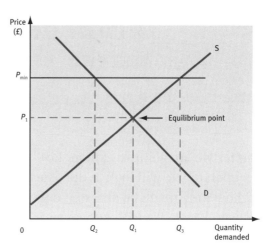

A good example of a minimum price is the national minimum wage. Another example is when governments intervene in agricultural markets to protect the income of farmers.

Maximum price

A maximum price is set below the equilibrium as shown in the diagram below.

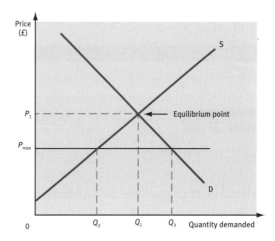

A maximum price means that the price is not allowed to rise above this level. At a maximum price of P_{max}, Q_2 would be supplied but Q_3 would be demanded, thus causing excess demand.

The effect of imposing a maximum price in the market is to leave demand unsatisfied. So who will get the product and who will not? It might be first come, first served, or some type of rationing system may be used (as during and after World War Two). In either case, demand is still left unsatisfied, so an unofficial market (black market) is likely to develop. For example, demand may outstrip supply for limited concert dates, and some tickets may be sold by touts, or on the internet, for inflated prices.

3 How do firms operate in competitive markets?

3.1 Costs, revenues and profit

In this chapter we are going to explore how businesses operate. We will look at the objectives of firms, and how they might be different depending on their size and type. We will then go on to look at costs, revenues and profit.

LEARNING OUTCOME:

The next two pages will help you to:

- identify business objectives, including profit
- identify and calculate fixed and variable, total and average costs
- identify and calculate total and average revenues
- identify and calculate profit.

AO1 and AO2 skills ACTIVITIES

Choose one public sector organisation and one private sector organisation. Using the internet, research each organisation's mission statement and objectives. How do they differ?

AO1 and AO2 skills ACTIVITIES

- List three suitable objectives for:
  a) a new small takeaway
  b) an established takeaway
  c) McDonald's.

- What are the main differences between the objectives?
- The National Health Service is owned and run by the government. How might objectives for the NHS differ from those you stated in answer to the first question?

Business objectives

An objective is a target that a business sets itself. Targets may be short-term or long-term. The main objective for most firms is profit maximisation.

Business objectives might include:

- to break even
- to increase market share
- to survive
- to make returns to shareholders (dividends)
- to increase sales
- to provide a good service.

Costs

When firms produce goods and services, they use resources (factors of production – land, labour, capital and enterprise). Firms must buy these resources.

Fixed costs are costs that do not vary with **output**, so if a firm produces zero units, it will have to pay exactly the same amount of fixed cost as if it produces 1000 units. Examples include rent, business rates and interest payments on loans.

Variable costs vary directly with output. If the firm produces more goods, then variable costs rise. Examples include production-line workers' wages and raw materials.

Total costs are all the costs of producing a good or service added together.

total costs = fixed costs + variable costs

Average costs are the total costs divided by the output.

average costs = total costs/output

ACTIVITIES *AO1 and AO2 skills*

Ben and James own a cookie shop. They make 1000 cookies per week. They have the following costs:

Rent	£1000 per week
Salaries	£1000 per week
Chocolate chips	25 p per cookie
Cookie mix	50 p per cookie
Electricity	£25 per 1000 cookies
Interest on loan	£50 per week

- State two fixed costs.
- State two variable costs.
- Calculate the fixed costs.
- Calculate the variable costs.
- Calculate total costs.
- Calculate average costs.

Revenue

When a firm produces a good or a service, the aim is to sell it. They set the price and consumers buy it. When a firm calculates the total amount of money it has received from selling a product, this is called **total revenue**.

total revenue = price × quantity sold

Average revenue is the total revenue divided by the output. This is the same as the price.

average revenue = total revenue/output

Profit

Profit is the total amount of money a firm makes after it has paid all its costs.

profit = total revenue – total costs

ACTIVITIES *AO1 and AO2 skills*

Ben and James decide to sell their cookies for £2 a cookie.

- If they sell 1000 cookies a week, calculate the total revenue made in one week.
- Calculate their profit (or loss).

APPLY IT!

US telecom group AT&T nearly tripled its profits in 2005, despite falling revenues. The rise in profits was thanks to cost-cutting measures. Profits increased from $108 million to $307 million. Cost-cutting measures included cutting 6100 jobs and abandoning some marketing.

Suggest other ways the company could have reduced costs.

3.2 Productivity

We will be looking at what productivity is and how we measure it. We shall also be discussing how to increase productivity, and why firms need to do this.

> **LEARNING OUTCOME:**
>
> The next two pages will help you to:
> - understand what is meant by productivity
> - explain the difference between production and productivity
> - explain how productivity may be increased by the specialisation of labour, the substitution of capital and worker involvement
> - explain and assess the impact of competitive forces on the need for increased productivity.

Productivity and production

Productivity and production are two very different concepts. **Production** is the process of combining scarce resources to produce an output (good or service).

Productivity is usually measured as output per worker per period of time (although it is also possible to measure the productivity of other factors of production, such as capital).

Assume a car factory employs 500 workers and produces 12 000 cars per year. The productivity of each worker is 12 000/500 = 24 cars per year. If another car factory employs more workers, but only produces the same amount of cars, then its labour productivity is lower.

Specialisation and productivity

Specialisation involves individuals, firms or countries producing only a limited range of goods or services. For example, your teacher has specialised in teaching economics; Apple has specialised in producing electronic goods. The UK could be said to have specialised in financial services.

By specialising in producing one product, a firm or individual can become better at producing that product, and so become more productive.

ACTIVITIES

Divide the class into companies of eight pupils. Each company will be producing gift tags. Each company will need the following: one pair of scissors, one pencil, one ruler, one rubber, one red pen and three sheets of plain paper.

Each gift tag should be 10 cm (width) by 7 cm (length). The tag must be folded in half to be 5 cm by 7 cm. On the front there should be a square measuring 2 cm by 2 cm (see diagram). Inside, the word 'To' must be written at the top left-hand side.

Each company must aim to make eight gift tags. Each tag must be exactly the same, and as per the instructions. The winning team will be the team that produces the most acceptable gift tags in the production period. Any gift tags that do not meet the strict quality control measures at the end of the production process will not count.

One team should be asked to organise a production line, with each person specialising in one part of the production process (one person cutting, one person drawing the square, etc.). Another team should be asked to organise the production process differently, with each individual producing one gift tag.

After production, when a winning team has emerged, discuss within your team what you did well, and what did not go well. With the whole class, discuss the advantages and disadvantages of specialisation.

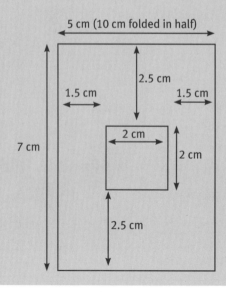

US workers were more productive than many analysts had forecast during the first three months of 2008. Productivity, or the total output per hour of work, rose at an annual rate of 2.2% in the first three months in 2008.

Analysts had expected an increase of closer to 1.5%. What might have led to this rise in productivity?

There are both advantages and disadvantages of specialisation.

Advantages	Disadvantages
Workers can be given jobs they are more suited to	Higher cost of training workers
Increased productivity	Boredom because workers are doing the same job every day
Lower average costs	Quality may suffer if workers become bored
Each worker can concentrate on what they are best at and build up expertise	Workers' skills may suffer
Higher pay for specialised workers	Workers may eventually be replaced by machinery
Improved skills at job	

How can firms increase productivity?

When firms use more capital (machinery) in the production process they are said to be capital-intensive. By using more capital in production, a firm may increase productivity because capital (machinery) can run continually without taking breaks, and so increase the amount produced in a certain period of time.

Productivity can also be increased by workers specialising in a particular part of the production process (as you did in the earlier task).

If workers are given more training, they can increase their productivity. This involves increasing your human capital (see page 4), perhaps by taking a new qualification, or being given training on a piece of machinery by another worker.

The impact of competition

Higher productivity can benefit a company in a competitive market in a number of ways.

Lower average costs

Increased productivity means a firm will produce more in the same period of time, so the average cost falls.

Lower, more competitive price

As average costs fall, a firm is able to offer customers a lower price, as it can still maintain its profit. In competitive markets this is very useful, as it is likely that more customers will be attracted.

Higher profits

As average costs fall, a firm is able to make a larger profit margin. It may choose to use some of this profit to reinvest in new machinery, which in turn may help to increase productivity further.

Sophie and Lydia own a curtain-making business – 'Drawn'. They employ 15 people to help make curtains. Lydia is concerned that her employees are not very productive and so average costs are rising, which is having an impact on their profits.

Sophie and Lydia have a meeting to discuss the methods they should use to improve their productivity. They have asked you, a business consultant, to help them decide how to improve their productivity.

Write a report detailing at least two ways which Sophie and Lydia could use to improve their workers' productivity. You must make a recommendation to Sophie and Lydia about what they should do.

3.3 Growth of firms

When we discussed the objectives of firms (page 32), we noted that the main objective of most firms is to maximise profit. This is why many firms choose to grow in size. The larger the firm, the more control it is likely to have over its market, and therefore the more profit it can make. Here we are going to look at how firms grow in size, and the benefits and costs of this growth.

(page 32)

LEARNING OUTCOME:

The next two pages will help you to:

- understand how and why firms grow in size
- discuss the costs and benefits of growth for a business
- understand and explain the gains from competitive markets for firms, consumers, etc.
- understand and explain the role and operation of the product market
- evaluate the benefits and limitations of the product market

---

AO2 skills ACTIVITIES

Using the internet, find examples of firms that have grown in size over time on their own. Also find examples of mergers and takeovers.

The role of firms in the product market

We have seen in earlier units that firms supply goods and services in order to satisfy consumer demand. If, for example, the demand for holidays in the Gambia rises, then, all other things being equal, the price will rise. Firms will see that providing such holidays will enable them to gain more profit, so they are willing to supply more. The free working of the market mechanism has ensured that consumers get more of those products for which demand rises. This is an enormous benefit to consumers, who are said to be 'sovereign' – they have consumer sovereignty.

In order to supply more of these products, the firms will need more resources. These could include land, labour and capital. There could, however, be limitations on their ability to increase the supply of products that are in greater demand. Some factors of production are said to be immobile, which means it is difficult for them to move between jobs. For example, firms may require highly trained, skilled labour, and there may not be any such extra labour available in the short run. Firms may also require more capital equipment. This, in turn, may require considerable investment, which can only produce the extra output needed in the long run.

How do firms grow?

Firms can grow in size both internally and externally.

- **Internal growth** is generated through increasing sales. To do this, a firm needs to buy new equipment or outlets or factories, buy in more labour, or market its products in a more effective way.

- **External growth** is achieved through a **merger** or **takeover**. This is where one firm joins together with another.

KEY TERMS

Merger – agreed coming together of two firms.

Takeover – when one firm seeks to take control of another (this can be either friendly or hostile).

Integration – this occurs when two firms come together through either a merger or a takeover.

External growth can take the form of vertical, horizontal or conglomerate **integration** (see the diagram on page 37).

(see the diagram on page 37).

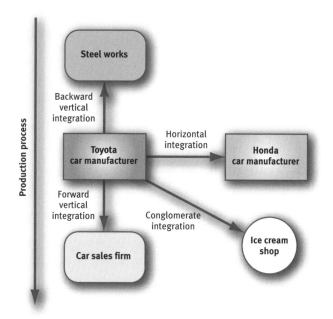

- it costs a lot of money to merge with or take over another business
- possibly less choice for customers in the market
- possibly higher prices to pay
- possible job losses and job insecurity
- possible diseconomies of scale.

Why do firms grow?

Most firms want to grow because they believe it will help them to increase their profit. Other reasons might be to increase brand image, to help reduce costs by achieving economies of scale, and to increase market power.

What are the costs and benefits of growth?

Benefits include:

- increased profits
- increased market share
- new ideas gained from the other business
- no competition with the other business
- gain from economies of scale
- the new business may not need all the workers.

Costs include:

- two sets of managers may not be able to agree
- the businesses may have different objectives and targets

FOR DEBATE

CO-OP 'FIFTH BIGGEST' AFTER SOMERFIELD BUYOUT

The Co-op returned to the big league of food retailing when its £1.6 billion takeover of rival Somerfield went through.

The deal – the biggest in its history – means the Co-op is the UK's fifth biggest food retailer, creating a chain of more than 3000 outlets with a market share of 8%.

Retail giant Tesco currently leads the way, with 31% of the UK's £120 billion grocery market, followed by Asda and Sainsbury's, with around 16%, and Morrisons, which has more than 11%.

16 July 2008, www.independent.co.uk

Read the article about supermarkets above and consider the following questions.

- What type of growth has occurred?
- What type of integration has occurred?
- Explain why Co-op would want to take over Somerfield.
- Discuss whether the takeover was the best way for Co-op to grow. Why?

APPLY IT!

Sophie and Lydia have decided that their curtain-making business, 'Drawn', needs to increase its market share. They have decided that they should buy another curtain-making business.

- Do you think this is the best option for Sophie and Lydia? Justify your answer.
- Do the advantages of taking over another business outweigh the costs to Lydia and Sophie?

3.4 Economies and diseconomies of scale

As discussed on pages 36–37, one of the reasons that firms choose to grow in size is because they can take advantage of economies of scale. Here we are going to explore how economies of scale occur, and how sometimes a firm can experience diseconomies of scale.

AO1 and AO2 skills ACTIVITIES

Fixit, a firm manufacturing tools, has calculated its total and average costs as follows.

Number of tools	Total costs (£)	Average costs (£)
1000	10 000	10
2000	18 000	9
3000	24 000	8
4000	28 000	7

- Draw a graph to show the relationship between the number of tools produced (*x* axis) and average costs (*y* axis).
- Explain what has happened to average costs as output has risen.

Economies of scale

As a firm grows larger in size (increases the number of products it produces), the long-run average costs fall.

Internal economies of scale occur when one firm grows in size.

There are six different types of internal economy of scale.

- **Risk-bearing** – as a firm grows larger, it is able to spread the risk over a larger number of outlets/factories/products.

- **Financial** – as a firm grows larger, it is able to obtain cheaper sources of finance. Banks are more willing to lend money to larger firms at a lower rate, because they are more likely to pay back the money.

- **Marketing** – larger firms will find it more cost-effective to advertise nationally.

- **Technical** – as a firm grows larger, it will be able to invest in machinery that can increase productivity and therefore lower the average cost of production.

- **Managerial** – as a firm grows larger, it is able to employ specialist managers, such as finance managers, to help make the workers more efficient.

- **Purchasing** – as a firm grows larger, it will be able to take advantage of price reductions from suppliers, as it can buy in bulk.

LEARNING TIP

A good way to remember the six types of economy of scale is the following mnemonic:

Really **F**un **M**ums **T**ry **M**aking **P**ies

KEY TERMS

Internal economies of scale – when one firm grows in size (increases output) and so benefits from lower average costs.

External economies of scale – when a whole industry grows in size, so a firm within that industry benefits from lower average costs.

External economies of scale occur when an industry grows. This may be because transport and communication links are improved, or local training and education opportunities become more focused on that industry.

ACTIVITIES

The firm Fixit, which manufactures tools, has calculated its total costs as follows.

Number of tools	Total costs (£)	Average costs (£)
1000	10 000	
2000	18 000	
3000	24 000	
4000	28 000	
5000	30 000	
6000	42 000	
7000	56 000	
8000	72 000	

- Calculate the average costs for each level of output.
- Which output produces the lowest average costs?
- Draw a graph to show the relationship between output of tools and the average costs.
- How would you describe the shape of this curve? Why is it this shape?

FOR DEBATE

In pairs, discuss what may have happened at Fixit to cause average costs to rise.

Diseconomies of scale

These occur when a firm grows too large and average costs start to rise.

Diseconomies of scale may occur for the following reasons.

- Loss of control – as a firm grows larger, it becomes more difficult to monitor all of its workers.
- Lack of co-ordination – it becomes more difficult to co-ordinate all aspects of the production process when a firm grows larger, especially if production spans a number of factories.
- Lack of co-operation – when a firm becomes larger, workers can feel alienated and lose motivation.

APPLY IT!

Delta and Northwest merger

In 2008 Delta Air Lines and Northwest Airlines argued their case to be allowed to create the world's biggest airline. The two airlines wanted to combine to create a single mega-airline called Delta.

They argued that the merger would create economies of scale to help offset oil prices that had topped $115 a barrel.

- State two types of economy of scale that the newly merged Delta Air Lines might benefit from.
- Explain how Delta Air Lines might benefit from these two economies of scale.
- Explain how Delta Air Lines might find itself experiencing diseconomies of scale.

3.5 Rewards for labour

So far, we have only really talked about *product* markets. We now turn our attention to a very important factor of production, labour, and the *labour* market. We will use the knowledge and understanding you developed previously with demand and supply and apply it to the labour markets.

Wage and salary

A wage is an individual payment, usually for a week's work. It tends to be given as an amount per hour.

A salary is an individual payment, usually for a month's work. It tends to be given as an amount per year, divided into 12 equal payments.

LEARNING OUTCOME:

The next two pages will help you to:

- understand and explain the role and operation of the labour market
- identify the differences between gross and net income, and between nominal and real income
- understand wage determination using simple demand-and-supply analysis.

AO2 skills ACTIVITIES

Using the information you collected in the previous Activity, list the jobs that earn a wage, and those that earn a salary.

Gross and net income

Gross income is the amount a person receives before all deductions are taken into account. Deductions include taxes such as income tax and national insurance, pension contributions and student loan repayments.

Net income is a person's take-home pay.

net income = gross income – deductions

Nominal and real income

Nominal income is the income paid to labour unadjusted for the effects of inflation.

Real income is the income paid to labour adjusted for the effects of inflation.

Inflation is a rise in the general level of prices of goods and services over a period of time (see page 62).

AO2 skills ACTIVITIES

Using an internet search engine, find out the level of wages for the following jobs: lifeguard, teacher, junior doctor, waitress, refuse collector, retail shop manager.

FOR DEBATE

In groups, discuss the differences in wages/salaries that you found in the Activity above.

- Why are there differences in the amount of pay?
- Why are some workers paid per hour and others paid a salary (yearly amount)?
- What 'perks' or bonuses do some workers receive?

APPLY IT!

Anna's earnings were £15 000 a year in 2007. In 2008, Anna's income rose by 4.5%, but this year inflation is 3%.

Anna's nominal income is now £15 675. But because of the effects of inflation, her income rose by only 1.5% in real terms.

The labour market

A labour market is the interaction between workers and employers. The market for labour is made up of the supply of labour (workers) and the demand for labour. Where demand and supply of labour meet, the market wage rate is determined (equilibrium wage rate).

How are wages determined?

Demand for labour is said to be a derived demand – this means that demand for labour is caused by the demand for the product, so if demand for the product increases, demand for labour also has to increase.

There is normally an inverse relationship between the demand for labour and the wage rate. This is because the higher the wage, the fewer workers an employer is likely to employ.

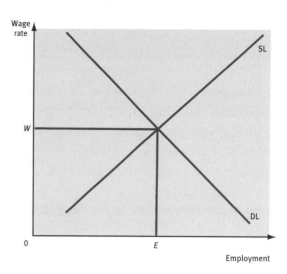

The supply of labour is the total number of workers willing to supply their labour at a given wage rate. The relationship between the wage offered and the supply of labour is positive. This is because as the wage rate rises, more people are willing to supply their labour.

The equilibrium wage rate is determined by the interaction of demand and supply, as shown in the diagram.

A change in either the demand for labour (DL) and/or the supply of labour (SL) will change the equilibrium, and cause a change in both the wage and the level of employment.

When labour demand increases (demand curve shifts right), there will be a rise in both wages and employment.

A rise in labour supply (supply curve shifts right) causes downward pressure on wages, although employment may increase.

When the wage rate is not at the market clearing level, a situation of disequilibrium exists. If wages lie above the equilibrium, there is an excess supply of labour, whereas an excess demand will occur when wages are below the equilibrium.

In January 2009, Dell confirmed that 1900 jobs would go at its Limerick plant over the next 12 months, after the firm decided to move its computer manufacturing operations to Poland.

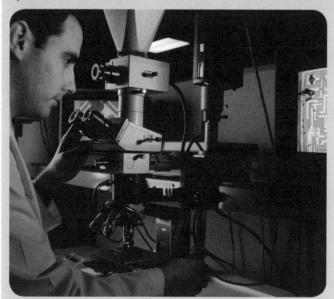

Dell said the move was part of a $3 billion initiative to cut costs following a review of its operations.

Suggest why this move enabled the company to cut its costs.

AO1 and AO2 skills ACTIVITIES

Explain, with the aid of a demand-and-supply diagram, how an economic recession might affect wages and employment in the car manufacturing industry.

3.6 Differences in wage rates

On pages 40 and 41, we learnt about how the labour market operates and what income is. We are now going to look at why there are differences in wage rates within and between occupations. We will also look at the national minimum wage in the UK.

LEARNING OUTCOME:

The next two pages will help you to:

- explain and evaluate wage differentials within and between occupations
- explain and evaluate the advantages and disadvantages of a national minimum wage.

ACTIVITIES

Using the internet, research the UK national minimum wage.

- When did the national minimum wage start in the UK?
- What is the current rate?
- Are there different rates for different people?
- How has the UK national minimum wage changed over time? (In what year do you think the photo was taken?)
- Why did the UK government decide to bring in a minimum wage?
- How does the minimum wage affect workers and firms?

Prepare a report on your findings.

Differences in wages within and between occupations

The main reasons for differences in the amounts people earn between industries and occupations are as follows.

- Differences in the productivity of workers – industries with high productivity will pay a higher average wage or salary.

- The elasticity of supply of labour (responsiveness of supply to a change in wage rates, see pages 26–27). The more inelastic the supply (supply is not very responsive to a change in wages), the higher the wage. Elasticity is affected by the skills, education and qualifications required for a particular job. A doctor's salary is high because the supply of doctors is fairly inelastic, due to the length of time it takes to train, and the number and high level of qualifications required.

- Trade union power – strong trade unions may be able to negotiate a mark-up on the wage through collective bargaining.

- Differences in the final demand for the product – earnings are higher in booming industries.

- Government pay policy – many public sector workers have their annual pay level determined by government-appointed pay review bodies. The government might hold down public sector pay to control its total spending and wage inflation in the economy.

- Compensating – higher pay may be a reward for risk-taking in certain jobs, for example for working in poor conditions and having to work unsocial hours.

- Different regional costs of living – it costs more to live in London than it does to live in Preston.

- Employer discrimination.

National minimum wage

The main aims of the **national minimum wage** are to reduce poverty and to reduce pay differentials between men and women. Other aims include reducing the exploitation of low-paid workers, and improving incentives for unemployed people actively to look for paid work.

Arguments for a minimum wage

- Higher tax revenue is received from the increased earnings of those in low-paid jobs.

- State benefits cost less – there is less need for benefit 'top-ups'.

- Income is more fairly distributed across the population.

- Poverty is reduced.

Arguments against a minimum wage

- It becomes more expensive to employ workers, so firms will cut jobs and unemployment will rise.

- Other workers will demand higher wages to maintain pay differentials.

- Higher wage costs will lead to rising inflation.

- Young and unskilled workers will lose out – firms will tend to employ older workers.

- Some firms may cut back on investment in worker training.

- A minimum wage will not ease poverty because many poor households do not have a low income-earner.

- It does not take into account regional differences in cost of living, so workers on the national minimum wage in London receive the same as workers on the national minimum wage in Sunderland.

Evaluating the national minimum wage

To evaluate the effects of the national minimum wage, we need to weigh up the advantages and disadvantages and decide which are the strongest arguments in particular circumstances.

The price elasticity of demand for workers is an important consideration. If the minimum wage is set above the equilibrium wage for an occupation, and the demand for those workers is elastic, then it will lead to a relatively large loss of jobs. Where demand for workers is inelastic, job losses will be fewer.

The price elasticity of supply of workers is also relevant. Where supply is elastic, the total unemployment caused by the minimum wage will be greater than where supply is inelastic. So a minimum wage set above the equilibrium wage could cause particularly high unemployment in occupations where the demand for, and supply of, labour is elastic. And the higher the minimum wage is set, the more dramatic its effects are likely to be.

There will be winners and losers. Workers who lose their jobs will suffer, while those who retain them at a higher wage rate will gain. We could ask, what is the point of raising the wage rate of some workers if it means they lose their jobs and end up with no wage at all?

One aim of the national minimum wage is to reduce poverty. But the poorest in society do not work, so this measure will have no effect on them. In fact, it will make the gap larger between the incomes of those who work and those who do not.

The overall effects on the economy of introducing a national minimum wage will depend on the state of the economy at the time. When UK introduced its minimum wage in 1999, the economy was in a period of steady economic growth and there were no major problems. Predictions of huge job losses did not prove correct, and the measure has generally been regarded as successful in guaranteeing a fair wage to the low-paid.

ACTIVITIES

A job advertisement for a teaching assistant in Blackpool offered £13 456.

- State and explain **two** factors that could lead to similar staff in London being offered £16 700.

- Explain **one** reason why workers whose price elasticity of supply is elastic are likely to be paid less than those with an inelastic supply.

ExamCafé

Welcome to the Exam Café for Part 1

Revision

Now that you have done all the work towards the exam, it's revision time. First of all, you need to know how you are going to be examined (page 47). Then you need to see some of the types of question you might be asked, and how you should answer them to get the best mark (pages 47–49). There are also sample exam questions on page 50.

REVISION TIP

A computer-based test!

When you take this exam don't worry that you may not have done an exam on the computer before. We are still testing your knowledge and understanding of economic concepts, so if you know what you are talking about with this unit you will do well.

REVISION TIP

Practise drawing the diagrams you will be including – the more you do this, the better they become, and the easier they will be to revise.

Always label every axis, curve and equilibrium (new and old). There are marks for all of these skills in an exam.

Common mistakes

Demand and supply – it is really important that you remember which way round demand and supply are. Every year, a handful of candidates lose marks because they have got them the wrong way round. Practise these diagrams every week.

Common mistakes

Always think about the **market situation** you are given – it's easy to become confused, especially if you are asked about substitute or complementary goods, as this can affect what happens to price and quantity sold.

REVISION TIP

Make sure you have learnt the basic calculations for costs, revenues and profit. In an exam, you may be asked to use information to calculate one of these.

REVISION TIP

It is really important that you learn all your economic concepts and practise your diagrams before the exam.

REVISION CHECKLIST – Part 1

	● Not confident ● Needs more revision ○ Confident		
	●	●	○
What is the economic problem?			
Factors of production			
Identify and understand examples of the four factors of production (land, labour, capital and enterprise).			
Scarcity, choice and opportunity cost			
Understand what is meant by the basic economic problem.			
Understand why and how choices are made.			
Apply the concept of opportunity cost to all economic decision-makers.			
Show an appreciation of how resources are allocated by individuals, firms and governments.			

	Not confident	Needs more revision	Confident	●	●	○

	●	●	○
Approaches to the economic problem			
Understand the meaning of primary, secondary and tertiary sectors.			
Identify and explain the key features of market and mixed economies.			
Identify and explain the key differences between public and private enterprises.			
Understand the meaning of specialisation.			
Evaluate the costs and benefits of specialisation.			
Explain how and why individuals, firms and countries specialise.			
Appreciate the use of money as a means of deferred payment, store of value, a unit of account and a medium of exchange.			
Explain and evaluate the costs and benefits of individuals/firms specialising.			
What are competitive markets?			
Markets			
Explain what is meant by a competitive market.			
Understand the implications for business(es) of operating in competitive markets.			
Explain the meaning of monopoly and monopoly power.			
Describe and evaluate the causes and consequences of monopoly power.			
Explain and evaluate the role of government in promoting competition.			
Demand			
Explain what is meant by demand.			
Construct an individual demand curve and a market demand curve from consumer data.			
Explain shifts of, and movements along, the demand curve.			
Understand the meaning of price elasticity of demand.			
Understand and construct graphs to illustrate price elasticity of demand.			
Understand the implications of price elasticity of demand for revenue.			
Supply			
Explain what is meant by supply.			
Construct an individual firm's supply curve and a market supply curve from production data.			
Explain shifts of, and movements along, the supply curve.			
Understand the meaning of price elasticity of supply.			
Understand and construct graphs to illustrate price elasticity of supply.			
Understand the implications of price elasticity of supply on businesses.			
Determination of price in competitive markets			
Understand how the interrelationship between market forces determines equilibrium price.			
Understand and explain the impact of competition on price.			
Explain and assess the effects of taxes and subsidies on price and quantity in competitive markets.			
Explain and assess the effects of maximum and minimum prices.			
How do firms operate in competitive markets?			
Costs, revenues and profit			
Identify business objectives, including profit.			
Identify and calculate total and average, fixed and variable costs.			
Identify and calculate total and average revenues.			
Identify and calculate profit.			

continued

Exam**Café**

	●	●	○
Productivity			
Understand what is meant by productivity.			
Explain the difference between production and productivity.			
Explain how productivity may be increased by the specialisation of labour, the substitution of capital and worker involvement.			
Explain and assess the impact of competitive forces on the need for increased productivity.			
Growth of firms			
Understand and explain the role and operation of the product market.			
Evaluate the benefits and limitations of the product market.			
Understand how and why firms grow in size.			
Explain internal and external economies and diseconomies of scale.			
Understand the implications and effects of internal and external economies of scale.			
Discuss the costs and benefits of growth for a business.			
Explain and assess the gains from competitive markets for firms, consumers, etc.			
Rewards for labour			
Understand and explain the role and operation of the labour market.			
Identify the differences between gross and net, and real and nominal income.			
Understand wage determination using simple demand and supply analysis.			
Explain and evaluate wage differentials within and between occupations.			
Explain and evaluate the advantages and disadvantages of a national minimum wage.			

REVISION MATRIX

Copy out and complete this revision matrix to identify factors that will cause shifts in the demand and supply curves.
(Some suggestions have been put in to get you started.)

	A rise in demand	**A fall in demand**	**A rise in supply**	**A fall in supply**
How is it defined?	Real incomes rise			
How is it measured?			Costs of production fall	
What are the causes?		A substitute good becomes cheaper		
What are the consequences?				An indirect tax is imposed

Exam Preparation

This exam will be a computer-based exam, one hour in length. There is a paper-based alternative for those for whom the computer test is unsuitable. This paper will consist of three sets of questions, 12 in total (four questions in each section). Each set of questions will be worth 20 marks. So the total paper is out of 60 marks. There will be some short-answer questions, some data-interpretation questions and some extended prose questions. All questions in this paper are compulsory. This exam will be worth 25% of your total GCSE Economics mark.

Understanding exam language

A big part of doing well in any exam is about understanding what the examiner wants from you in every question. To do this, you need to understand the command words they use. The number of marks available in a question provides a guide about how much, and at what level, to write.

> **Question 1. Explain** what is meant by specialisation. *(2 marks)*
>
> **Question 2.** The benefits of specialisation are greater than the costs. Do you agree? **Give reasons** for your answer. *(8 marks)*
>
> Both questions are asking about specialisation – but that is where the similarities end. The first point to notice is that question 1 is worth 2 marks, whereas question 2 is worth 8 marks. So you must write considerably more for question 2.
>
> The **command words** should also alert you to what the examiner wants.
>
> The command word in question 1 is **explain** – this means you must show your understanding of the term or theory being tested. The depth of explanation required is indicated by the mark allocation. Giving a well chosen example will often gain a mark.
>
> Question 2 is asking you to **discuss** – we know this because of the phrase 'give reasons for your answer'. 'Discuss' means put forward both sides of a case before coming to a brief conclusion. Discussion would require continuous writing.

Sample questions

> 1 Richard Branson thinks that entrepreneurs are an essential part of the economy. Do you agree? Give reasons for your answer. *(8 marks)*

Raj's answer

> An entrepreneur is someone who decides to set up a new business risking his/her own money and ideas. Entrepreneurs are essential for an economy as they are one way of allocating resources in an economy. They provide money for companies to expand and invest. Without entrepreneurs there would not be many new small firms entering the market, which creates more competition. This is beneficial to consumers.
>
> Not all entrepreneurs' ideas work, which can waste resources.

Examiner says: The student starts their answer well by defining entrepreneur.

Examiner says: This student's answer is good because they have looked at the argument both for and against entrepreneurs. However, the argument against is a little brief. This answer would achieve the top response level because they analysed both sides of the argument.

2 Using the demand diagram below, explain the effect on price and quantity sold of cars due to a rise in world oil prices. *(6 marks)*

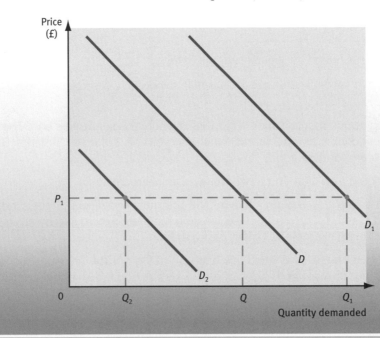

Examiner says: This is a good answer – the candidate has explained what the relationship is between oil and cars. They then go on to explain how it will affect the demand curve and then what happens to price and quantity sold.

Frances's answer

Cars and oil are complementary goods. This means that if you use a car you need oil (petrol) to be able to use it. So if the price of oil rises people will buy fewer cars because it becomes more expensive to use them. This means demand will fall for cars therefore shifting the demand curve to the left. The price of cars will fall and the quantity sold will also fall.

3 Are the benefits of competitive markets greater than the costs? Give reasons for your answer. *(8 marks)*

Nina's answer

A competitive market is one where lots of firms are present and competing for custom. Firstly this will drive down price as each firm tries to undercut the other to gain more customers. This is very beneficial to the consumer.

Another way firms will try to compete to attract customers is by improving their product range and its quality. Again this is beneficial to consumers as they can get the best products and have more choice. These two reasons are benefits for consumers.

Firms may not benefit from competition because it is likely their profits will fall as they have to drive their prices down. However, competition may be beneficial to firms in the long run because it forces them to become more productive, which means their average costs will fall and in the long run their profits might rise.

Examiner says: This is a good answer – the candidate looks at both consumers and producers.

4 Should pop and rock singers like Girls Aloud receive higher incomes than workers in jobs like nursing? *(8 marks)*

Frances's answer

The supply of nurses is much higher that the supply of pop singers like Girls Aloud, there is only one of them. The comparatively small number of decent singers like Girls Aloud drives up the wages. There is a much greater supply of nurses available.

The demand for Girls Aloud is very high and because they are the only people who can satisfy that demand they can demand a higher wage. Girls Aloud can also generate large amounts of money for their record company. However it could be argued that the difference in wages is excessive.

Examiner says: A good answer, which briefly explains a number of reasons why Girls Aloud receive a higher income than nurses. The candidate briefly recognises the other side of the argument at the end.

Sample exam questions (Part 1)

1 Allan and Jim each have £50 spending money. Jim has decided he is going to save his money in the bank. Allan is unsure what he is going to do with his money. Allan really wants a new shirt for work, which costs £50, and he would also like to buy a some books which cost £40.

(a) Explain what is meant by the basic economic problem. (2)

(b) Explain what is meant by the term resources. (2)

(c) With the help of the information above, explain how needs and wants are different. (4)

(d) Explain, using the example above, what is meant by opportunity cost. (4)

2 Rosie works 25 hours a week at a cake shop, 'Occasions', for which she is paid the minimum wage. Occasions is a private business. Rosie enjoys her job, and works very hard. In one day she can make five cakes. Janet also works at Occasions, she can make seven cakes a day.

(a) State two objectives a firm like Occasions might have. (2)

(b) Using the information above, explain what is meant by:

(i) production (2)

(ii) productivity. (2)

(c) With reference to the information above, explain how productivity may be increased by specialisation. (6)

(d) Occasions operates in a competitive market. To what extent will operating in a competitive market mean that Occasions needs to increase productivity in order to compete? (8)

3 Damien is a teaching assistant. His incomplete payslip is below:

Payments (£)		Deductions (£)			
Description	Amount	Tax	156.40		
Basic pay	1312.07	NI	79.74		
		Pension	77.41		
Total payments	1312.07	Total deductions		Net pay	

(a) Using the information in the payslip, calculate (showing your working):

(i) total deductions
(ii) net pay (2)

(b) Using the payslip, explain what is meant by gross pay. (2)

(c) Explain two reasons why Damien, who is a teaching assistant, earns less than Tim, who is a doctor. (6)

(d) The government introduced the National Minimum Wage in 1997 to help reduce the differentials between lower-paid and higher-paid jobs. Do you agree that the National Minimum Wage is beneficial to workers? Give reasons for your answer. (8)

4 A:

> **UK government increase tax on aviation fuel**

B:

> **UK SUMMER SET TO BE HOT!**

C:

> **INTEREST RATES AT LOWEST FOR OVER 50 YEARS**

(a) Explain what is meant by supply. (2)

(b) With the aid of a demand-and-supply diagram, explain why an increase in aviation fuel (headline A) will cause the price of travel to the UK to rise, and the quantity demanded to fall. (4)

(c) Choose either headline B or C and, with the aid of a demand-and-supply diagram, explain how it might affect the market for UK tourism. (6)

RYANAIR ANNOUNCES PLANS FOR STANDING TICKETS

Ryanair has put forward a proposal to allow willing passengers to 'stand' on short flights for a cheaper ticket.

The idea involves taking out the back five or six rows of seats and putting in 'vertical seating'. This could mean Ryanair can increase passenger numbers by 40% on each plane and cut its costs by 20%.

(d) To what extent is this the best way for Ryanair to compete with other airlines? Give reasons for your answer. (8)

Answers and mark schemes are available online, go to www.heinemann.co.uk

Part 2 How the economy works

How is the UK economy getting on? Is it performing well or badly?

When you see these questions, what exactly are they asking about? There are four major economic variables to consider when we are discussing 'the economy', and we will find out what they are in this part of the book.

There has to be a general election in the UK every five years, although they are often more frequent than this. What decides which political party a person votes for? More often than not, it is economic factors which decide how people vote. If the current government has managed a healthy economy then it has a very good chance of being re-elected. On the other hand, if people consider the economy to be 'in a mess', they may vote against the current government. Which factors do people consider when deciding who to vote for?

The UK economy is a mixed economy. This means it is based on a market economy, but the government (the state) also takes an active role.

In a pure market economy there is no government intervention. Firms and households are just left to 'get on with it'. The owners of the firms will be driven by the profit motive: profit is their incentive to do well. Nobody will take responsibility for the economy as a whole.

In a mixed economy, the government actively participates. The UK government provides a range of services, including health, education and defence. It also undertakes to manage the economy as a whole. This means it operates policies in order to achieve its objectives for the economy.

An economy can be considered to be doing well when it has close to full employment, a sound rate of economic growth, low inflation and healthy balance of payments. This matches the objectives of the government to:

- maintain full employment
- achieve economic growth
- ensure price stability
- balance exports and imports.

In this part of the book, we consider employment (and unemployment), economic growth and inflation in some detail. The balance of payments (the balance between exports and imports) is considered in Part 3.

A fifth objective of government is to reduce inequalities of income. In Chapter 5 we explain what this means and how it is achieved.

As the UK is a mixed economy, a large part of its output is in the public sector. This has to be financed somehow, and a lot of the revenue comes from taxation. In these chapters we will also find out what the main areas of government spending are, and where the tax revenue comes from to finance this expenditure.

4 What are the economic objectives of the government?
4.1 Objectives of government policy

Macro-economics is the study of the whole economy. We all live in the economy, so how it is performing does affect us all. The four major aspects of the economy concern employment, economic growth, inflation and the balance of payments. So the objectives of government policies are related to these four variables.

What are the objectives of government policy?

The four main macro-economic objectives of government are shown in the diagram.

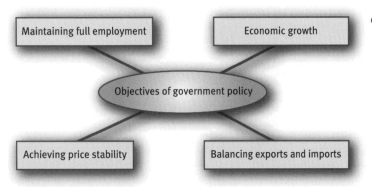

Full employment

Full employment means that everyone who is able and willing to work has a job. This does not mean that everyone of working age has a job. Many choose to stay at home to care for their children; others retire early; and others continue in education for a few years. The workforce includes only those who are working plus the unemployed who are looking for a job. In practice, the government does not aim for 100% employment, as there must be people who are between jobs at any one time (see page 59). When the government achieves high employment and low unemployment, this increases the welfare of society.

Economic growth

Economic growth refers to growth of output in the economy. The value of output will be equal to the value of the incomes for the workers and owners of **factors of production** which produce that output. Thus the government is aiming for a more affluent (richer) economy.

> ### KEY TERM
> **Factors of production** – resources comprising land (including natural resources), labour, capital and enterprise.

The government would like to achieve a steady rate of growth, illustrated as the trend rate of growth in the graph below. The government would like to

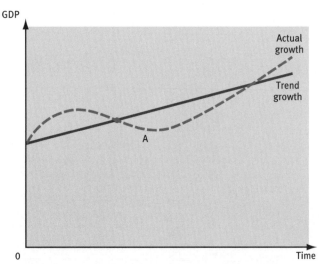

avoid cyclical changes in the gross domestic product (GDP) (see page 54) as illustrated by the actual growth line. This pattern is known as the economic cycle. In particular, the government wishes to avoid a period like that marked A in the diagram. This is a recession.

Price stability

Price stability means keeping inflation low. Inflation is the rise in the general price level. As we shall see, inflation can have serious disadvantages for the economy, especially high rates of inflation. In practice, the UK government does not aim for zero inflation, but for a low rate of 2% per annum.

Balancing exports and imports

The government aims for a balance between exports and imports over time. This does not mean that the value of exports should equal the value of imports each year – but that deficits in some years should be matched by surpluses in other years. This is considered in more detail in Part 3.

What are the policies of government?

The government has three main policies to try to achieve its macro-economic aims, as shown in the diagram.

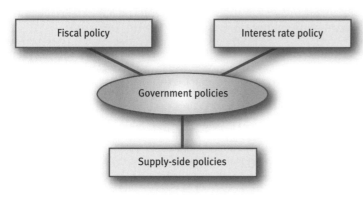

Fiscal policy

Fiscal policy is aimed at changing the level of total (aggregate) demand in the economy through changes in taxation and the government's own spending. If the objective is to achieve more employment and economic growth, then the government will operate a fiscal policy to raise total (aggregate) demand. On the other hand, if the objective is to achieve a lower rate of inflation and reduce imports/increase exports, then it will operate a fiscal policy to reduce total (aggregate) demand.

Interest rate policy

Interest rate policy is also aimed at changing the level of total (aggregate) demand in the economy, but through changes in interest rates. This policy is not operated directly by the government, but by the Bank of England (which has been given this responsibility by the government). If the objective is to achieve more employment and economic growth, then the Bank of England will reduce interest rates to raise total (aggregate) demand. On the other hand, if the objective is to achieve a lower rate of inflation and reduce imports/increase exports, then it will raise interest rates to reduce total (aggregate) demand.

Supply-side policies

Supply-side policies are not aimed at the demand side of the economy. They aim to increase the economy's capacity to produce more goods and services. These policies can help the government to achieve all four of its macro-economic objectives.

An example would be education and training, which would improve the quality of the workforce.

Combining these policies

The government is able to use a combination of policies to achieve an objective. If the government wishes to raise employment and reduce unemployment, it can increase government spending and lower taxes through its fiscal policy. The Bank of England can reduce interest rates at the same time. Both of these policy measures will increase total (aggregate) demand in the economy. In addition, the government could use supply-side policies, such as education and training, to help people to gain employment.

AO1 and AO2 skills ACTIVITIES

The Treasury updates its website twice a year, summarising the Budget or the pre-Budget report. Print out the summary of the latest Budget or pre-Budget report, and highlight any references to the government's objectives or policies.

4.2 Economic growth

Why is it that material living standards are a lot higher today than when your parents and grandparents were young? The answer is – **economic growth**. The country's output has grown over time, so there are more goods and services to consume.

ACTIVITIES

When an economy grows, it means there are more goods and services available for its citizens. Write down all the things that you and your household consume, that you believe your grandparents did not consume when they were your age. Then ask a grandparent if your list is accurate. He or she will probably be able to add to it. Are there items that they consumed but you do not?

KEY TERMS

Economic growth – growth in output of the economy over time – a growth of real GDP over time.

Gross domestic product (GDP) – the total value of goods and services produced in the country in a year.

GDP per capita – GDP divided by the total population, therefore GDP per head.

What is economic growth?

Economic growth is growth of the country's output over time. Output is usually measured as **gross domestic product (GDP)**, the value of all the goods and services produced within the country in a year. This is the same as the total incomes of the people of the country in a year. The total value of output becomes incomes for those who produce it – incomes in the form of wages, profits, interest and rent.

How is economic growth measured?

The government measures the value of the country's output and calculates the rate at which it has risen. For example, if in year 1 the GDP was £500 billion, and in year 2 it had grown to £510 billion, then it would have grown by £10 billion, which is 2% more than £500 billion. The economic growth rate was 2%.

This assumes there was no inflation. In practice, inflation has to be deducted to measure growth of GDP in real terms. For example, if money GDP grew by 5% but the inflation rate was 3%, then real GDP growth was 5 – 3 = 2%.

ACTIVITIES

Calculate the economic growth rate in the following cases. (Assume no inflation.) Use the formula:

change in GDP/original GDP × 100

GDP (£ billion)		Economic growth rate (%)
In year 1	In year 2	
100	103	
200	202	
300	312	

What is GDP per capita?

GDP per capita is GDP divided by the population. This is also called GDP per head, because it is the average output (or income) which each person in the country has. It is important to stress that this is only an average figure – the actual GDP will be distributed unevenly. This is considered in more detail on pages 70–71.

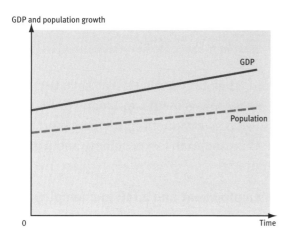

GDP and population growth

The graph shows that if GDP grows faster than the population, then GDP per capita will rise.

AO2 skills **ACTIVITIES**

Calculate GDP per capita in the following cases (£1 billion = £1000 million).

GDP (£ billion)	Population (million)	GDP per capita
600	60	
800	40	
500	12.5	

The following graph shows UK's annual rate of economic growth over recent years.

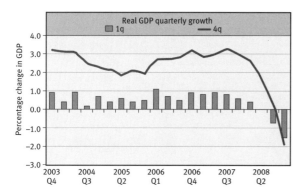

Real GDP quarterly growth

(Source: www.statistics.gov.uk)

AO1 and AO2 skills **ACTIVITIES**

- Use the internet to find out UK's current GDP and GDP per capita.
- What have the growth rates been like over your lifetime?

What are the causes of economic growth?

Resources, known as **factors of production** (see page 52), are needed in order to produce goods and services. The quantity and quality of factors of production are very important in affecting the rate of economic growth. We will consider some of these below.

- **Investment** – spending on capital goods, such as premises, machinery and equipment. More investment means the economy has the capacity to produce more goods and services in the future.

- **Changes in technology** – technical progress means the quality of capital goods improves, and a given quantity of capital can now produce more output than before.

- **A larger workforce** – the economy can produce more if it has more workers. There may be a natural increase in the working population (e.g. more school-leavers), or immigration may bring more workers. A lot of workers came to the UK from Eastern Europe in the decade from 1999.

- **Education and training** – this affects the quality of the workforce. The more educated, trained and skilled the workers, the higher the output of the country is likely to be.

- **Natural resources** – if a country discovers or develops natural resources, this can be a stimulus to economic growth. This has been a very important factor affecting the development of some Middle Eastern countries where large oilfields have been exploited. The discovery and exploitation of North Sea oil has increased UK's economic growth rate over the years.

- **Government policies** – the government takes responsibility for the macro-economic management of the economy. The effectiveness of government policies can have a significant bearing on the economic growth rate (see pages 52–53).

Evaluating the causes of economic growth

This means trying to judge which of the above factors are the most important in any particular case. For example, the discovery and development of oilfields may have been one of the most important factors influencing the growth of Kuwait's economy, whereas a large amount of capital investment has played a very important role in China's development in recent times. Increasing the economy's capacity to produce alone may not lead to a rise in real GDP unless the demand for its goods and services is also rising.

4.3 Costs and benefits of economic growth

Economic growth is a major objective of government policy. This implies that it must have benefits which outweigh any costs. We will consider this issue further in this chapter.

LEARNING OUTCOME:

The next two pages will help you to:

- identify and explain the benefits and costs of economic growth
- evaluate whether the benefits outweigh the costs.

ACTIVITIES

An average 15-year-old in an African country such as Kenya consumes much less than an average 15-year-old in the UK.

Make a list of things that you and your family consume, that you believe are unlikely to be consumed by the average-income family in Kenya.

Benefits of economic growth

A rise in material living standards

If GDP rises at a faster rate than the population, the GDP per capita rises. This means everyone, on average, has more output available to consume than before. They are materially better off. For example, between 1992 and 2008, the UK had 16 years of uninterrupted economic growth and its citizens became richer. We took more holidays abroad, ate out at pubs and restaurants more, and bought better consumer durables for our homes, such as flat-screen televisions and computers with broadband.

A rise in the welfare of the population

As the capacity of the economy to produce more grows, the government is able to devote more resources to services such as health and education. This can improve the general welfare of the country. This is especially beneficial to developing countries, enabling their citizens to have greater access to health and education services that have been lacking. Economic growth can mean very important progress, such as a reduction in infant mortality rates, an increase in life expectancy, and a greater rate of literacy.

A rise in employment and a fall in unemployment

As output rises, more workers will be required to produce it, and the unemployment rate will fall.

A reduction in poverty

As output and incomes rise, the government is able to take more in taxes from the higher-income groups and use the revenue to raise the living standards of those with lower incomes, for example by providing benefits.

Costs of economic growth

Environmental costs

Greater output and consumption can lead to more pollution of the land, air, sea and fresh water, as well as noise pollution. For example, more road transport leads to more air and noise pollution. The greater output achieved worldwide has led to global warming. Many people believe this will have significant adverse effects on the environment, such as a rise in sea levels.

Congestion

Economic growth is often concentrated in certain urban areas, which can become overcrowded and congested. There may be pressure on services such as hospitals, schools and public transport. Roads tend to become more congested and travelling times increase.

Loss of non-renewable resources

Economic growth uses resources that can't be replaced, including oil, natural gas, metals and other minerals. This argument also applies to natural environments such as rainforests. As trees are cut down to increase the output of timber, and palm oil plantations replace the rainforest, many animals and plants become endangered and some face extinction.

A lower quality of life

We have seen that growth makes people materially better off. However, it can change people's lifestyles, sometimes to their disadvantage. They may move from the countryside to cities and lead a more stressful life.

Inequalities of income and wealth

The benefits of growth are unevenly spread. This means some people become better off, while others are 'left behind'. The gap between rich and poor becomes wider.

Inflation

Sometimes the rate of economic growth is too fast for the economy to respond without a rise in the general price level.

Evaluating the consequences of economic growth

Do the benefits of economic growth outweigh the costs?

There is no right or wrong answer to this question. We have to weigh up the arguments for and against economic growth. In a poor developing country, the benefits of economic growth are fairly obvious. It could enable people to have a better diet and access to clean drinking water and medical facilities, and more children to go to school for more years. China has had rapid economic growth in recent years, so many of its citizens are better off than a generation ago. They have a wider variety of food and clothes, more consumer goods, and so on.

But for a developed economy such as the UK, the benefits of growth may be less obvious. The citizens still seem to want the material benefits which growth brings, such as satnav systems, the latest computer game consoles and games, and new cars. They also place ever greater demands on health services, which are more likely to be met if there is economic growth. On the other hand, problems linked to growth increase. For example, there are more obese people, including children, than ever before as economies such as UK's and USA's have grown. And there is more pollution, as well as other environmental costs.

Some environmentalists argue against economic growth, for the reasons given above. But others argue that the extra resources brought about by economic growth could be used to help the environment, for example by purchasing and maintaining nature reserves.

Quality of life

Quality of life does not just depend on material possessions and consumption. It takes account of factors such as our amount of leisure time and the quality of the environment in which we work and live.

FOR DEBATE

Does economic growth improve quality of life? We would expect it to do so in poor countries, where people do not have enough basic necessities such as clean water, food, health services and education. What about in a country like the UK? Are people of your age any happier now than they were 25 or 50 years ago? Material living standards have undoubtedly risen; but are people any happier?

AO1, AO2 and AO3 skills   ACTIVITIES

More economic growth means more sources of energy are needed. Reserves of non-renewable oil, gas and coal will become more depleted. Working in groups, can you suggest alternative sources of energy? For each suggestion, can you give some arguments both for and against using more of those types of energy?

4.4 Employment and unemployment

Most households in the UK receive most of their income in the form of wages and salaries. They rely on employment for their income. To maintain a high level of employment and low unemployment is a major aim of government policy.

LEARNING OUTCOME:

The next four pages will help you to:

- understand what is meant by employment and unemployment
- explain how unemployment is measured
- identify types of unemployment and explain their causes
- explain and evaluate the consequences of unemployment.

AO1 skills **ACTIVITIES**

How many people are employed in the UK? How many are unemployed? What is the rate of unemployment? If you go to www.statistics.gov.uk you can find out the answers to these questions and see the recent employment and unemployment trends.

KEY TERMS

Full employment – when all those able and willing to work are in paid employment at the current wage rate.

Unemployment – when workers who are able and willing to work are unable to find employment (at current wage rates).

Employment and unemployment

Employment refers to the employment of labour in the economy. Most households rely on employment for most of their income (in the form of wages).

Full employment occurs when an economy is using all of its workforce. In practice, this does not mean 100% employment because there will always be some people who are between jobs. Some industries will be declining and jobs will be lost, at the same time as others are expanding and require more workers. So it is necessary that some people move between jobs, and there will be time lags when this happens.

Unemployment occurs when workers who are able and willing to work at the current wage rates are unable to find employment. These people are part of the workforce although they are not presently in work. People who are not seeking work, such as retired people, full-time students and those who choose to be housewives or househusbands, are not part of the workforce and are not counted as unemployed.

The graph shows UK employment over a number of years.

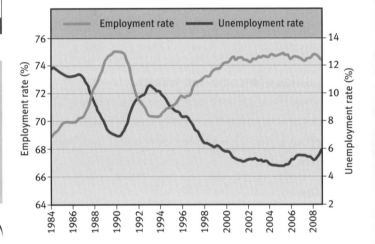

Measuring unemployment

There are two ways of measuring unemployment which are used by the government: the **claimant count**, and the **Labour Force Survey**.

KEY TERMS

Claimant count – measures unemployment according to the number of people claiming unemployment-related benefits (such as Jobseeker's Allowance).

Labour Force Survey – a survey of a sample of households, counting people as unemployed if they are actively seeking work but do not have a job (in the week of the survey).

The Labour Force Survey uses standard International Labour Organization methods of measuring unemployment, so the figures are directly comparable with those of other countries using the same method. In practice, the Survey method gives a much larger figure for total unemployment than the claimant count method. This must be because some people who are without a job and are seeking work are not claiming benefits at a Job Centre.

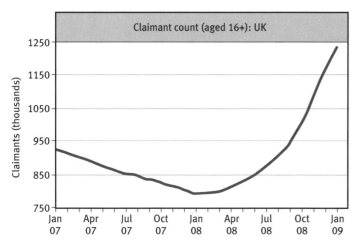

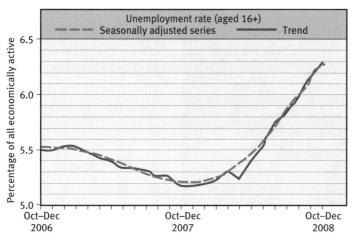

(Source: www.statistics.gov.uk)

The two graphs show UK unemployment over a number of years, as measured by the two methods.

What are the types and causes of unemployment?

Voluntary unemployment

This is caused by people choosing not to work. For example, a person who is made redundant from an £800 per week job may choose not to take up another job if the only jobs available are paying £400 a week or less. Voluntary unemployment may depend on the social protection system. It is often argued that state benefits are too generous, so people may prefer to claim benefits than to work. The after-tax income from work may not be much larger than the income from benefits, so people may choose to remain voluntarily unemployed.

Seasonal unemployment

This is caused by seasonal workers not being employed at other times of year, for example in the tourist industry. In the UK, coastal resorts tend to employ many workers in the summer months only.

Frictional unemployment

This is caused by workers moving between jobs. There are time lags between workers leaving their job and starting a new one.

Structural unemployment

This is caused by long-term changes in the structure of industry when some industries decline. This is a serious, long-term type of unemployment. The workers are often occupationally immobile, which means they have the wrong skills and qualifications for other jobs. They are also geographically immobile – they find it difficult to move to where new jobs are located.

Technological unemployment

This is caused by capital taking the place of labour. Automation means that workers lose their jobs. This has been common in manufacturing industries, for example the increased use of robots on car assembly lines. It also applies in service industries, for example the increase in internet banking reduces the need for bank workers in local branches.

Cyclical unemployment

This is caused by a fall in total (aggregate) demand in the economy (see page 53). If the demand for goods and services falls, then fewer workers are needed to produce the output, and some will be laid off. These unemployed now have lower incomes, and in turn they will spend less. This means producers face a further cut in incomes and will lay off more workers. This process continues in a vicious cycle, and can lead to very high levels of unemployment – mass unemployment.

AO1 and AO2 skills **ACTIVITIES**

During 2007 and 2008, there were major problems in the financial sectors of the economies of UK, USA and other countries. Some financial institutions (banks, insurance companies, etc.) went bust, while others were taken over. Do some research to find out which banks and organisations were most affected. They included well known names from the UK high street. Which type of unemployment did this lead to?

What are the consequences of unemployment?

A thriving economy does need to have some frictional unemployment, because it needs people to move between jobs. Patterns of demand change, so the demand for some products, and thus for the workers to produce them, will fall. Meanwhile, the demand for new products rises, and the economy will need workers to produce these. So it essential that some people change jobs, and there is likely to be some unemployment in the meantime. It is important to realise that, over time, with frictional unemployment, different people are unemployed for a short time each, rather than the same people being long-term unemployed.

The consequences of other types of unemployment are mostly unfavourable to the economy.

Labour resources are wasted

The economy is not using all of its resources to full capacity. This means that the economy could produce more goods and services than it is currently producing – which is a waste of resources.

Lower living standards

Workers and their families suffer a lower standard of living as unemployment causes their incomes to fall.

Excluded workers

Some people are unemployed for so long that they become excluded from the workforce. They become unemployable. Employers are reluctant to take them on, and they eventually give up looking for work altogether.

Costs to taxpayers

The unemployed are entitled to Jobseeker's Allowance or other benefits. The more unemployed people there are, the greater the cost to taxpayers. In fact, those still in work may have to pay higher taxes to support the increased number of unemployed.

A budget deficit

As well as the rise in spending on benefits explained above, the government loses tax revenue from workers when they become unemployed, for example in the form of income tax and national insurance contributions that will not be received. Spending in the economy will fall, and the government will receive even less tax revenue. So the government's budget is likely to fall into deficit. (We will see later, however, that this deficit can help to combat unemployment – see page 76.)

Regional problems

Unemployment is unlikely to be spread evenly throughout the country. In times of high unemployment some locations tend to suffer much more than others, and may become 'depressed areas'. Unemployment in these regions is well above the national average, and the lack of demand in the area leads to even more unemployment. Some people may move away and the local population declines.

Social problems

As well as lower living standards, the unemployed may suffer from a loss of status and self-esteem. Unemployment can contribute to problems such as marital break-up. It may also lead to other social problems, including an increased crime rate.

Evaluating the consequences of unemployment

In order to do this, it is necessary to weigh up the costs and the benefits. As we have seen, some frictional unemployment is necessary for a healthy economy which adapts to changes over time. Other types of unemployment are usually considered to impose costs on the economy, and these are explained above. As unemployment causes serious problems for the economy and its citizens, achieving a high level of employment and a low level of unemployment are major aims of government policies. How the government attempts to achieve these aims is considered in more detail in Chapter 6.

APPLY IT!

General Motors (GM) was one of the largest companies in America, and the largest motor company in the world. Its brands included Buick, Cadillac, Chevrolet, Hummer, Pontiac, Saab, Vauxhall, Opel and Daewoo. However, it was not only overtaken by Toyota as the largest car firm, it became inefficient and made large losses. In June 2009 GM filed for bankruptcy.

At one time, GM had employed 350 000 workers at 150 assembly plants. At the start of 2009 it still employed over 265 000 workers. Although GM will probably survive as a smaller business (the US government bailed it out), the bankruptcy will mean a huge rise in unemployment. Jobs will be lost not only in the car factories themselves, but also in the firms that supply materials and components.

TAKING IT FURTHER

The UK economy entered recession in mid-2008. In recession there is cyclical unemployment (see page 59), so we would expect UK unemployment to rise significantly during 2008 and 2009.

Was this the case? Go to www.statistics.gov.uk/hub/labour-market/people-not-in-work/unemployment/index.html to find out what happened to the unemployment rate during this period.

4.5 Inflation

We all have to pay the price when we buy our goods and services. How do we feel if the prices go up? Some prices receive a lot of attention in the news, including petrol, gas, electricity, housing and food. What is happening to prices in the UK at the moment?

LEARNING OUTCOME:

The next two pages will help you to:

- understand what is meant by price stability, inflation and the rate of inflation
- understand how the rate of inflation can be measured
- identify and explain the causes of inflation.

What is inflation?

KEY TERMS

Inflation – a sustained rise in the general price level over time.

Price stability – the general level of prices is kept constant or grows at an acceptably low rate over time.

Rate of inflation – the rate at which the general price level rises over time.

Inflation

Inflation is when prices rise. It is not the rise in price of one or two items – it is when all prices in general rise. When the price level rises for the goods and services that consumers buy, this means their money (e.g. £10) will not purchase as much as before. Therefore inflation could also be defined as a fall in the value of money – the purchasing power of money falls. This also means that the cost of living goes up – it costs people more to buy the same goods and services. Note that during a period of inflation it is still possible for the prices of some individual items to fall. For example, in recent years in the UK the prices of goods such as clothing and DVD players have fallen, even though the rate of inflation was positive.

Price stability

If prices are stable, this strictly means that they do not rise or fall at all. The UK government has the major objective of **price stability** for the economy. In practice, this does not mean zero inflation. Rather, the government sets a target of 2% per annum for the inflation rate.

The rate of inflation

The **rate of inflation** is the rate at which the general level of prices is rising over time. This is usually expressed as an annual rate. Thus if the price level is 2% higher on 1 January 2010 than on 1 January 2009, then the rate of inflation for 2009 was 2%.

How is inflation measured?

There are various measures of inflation, but the most prominent is the **Consumer Prices Index (CPI)**. This is the official measure of the rate of inflation for both the UK government and governments of other European Union countries.

The government finds out the spending pattern of average families in the country. It records the prices of everything families buy each month. This is done at hundreds of different retail outlets (supermarkets, etc.) across the country. So if prices rise from one month to the next, this is recorded in the CPI. The goods and services are weighted – those that take a higher proportion of the spending of families are more important in measuring the rate of inflation.

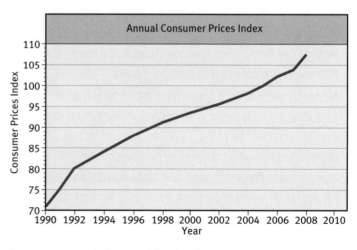

(Source: www.statistics.gov.uk/statbase)

A rise in the price of food in general, for example, would have more impact on the rate of inflation than a similar rise in the price of books. The index is given the number 100 at the start of the period. If, for example, the index becomes 103 after one year, then this reflects an inflation rate of 3% per annum. The prices of the goods and services bought by average families have risen by 3% overall.

The diagram shows the UK's rise in the general price level in recent years, as measured by the CPI.

ACTIVITIES

Using the internet, find out the prices of a range of items in the past. These could include a loaf of bread, a pint of milk, a TV licence, a laptop computer, or any other item you choose. You could split into groups and each person finds the prices for a particular item for 10, 20, 30, 40 and 50 years ago. Compare your findings for the various products. To get you started, look at petrol prices for the past 25 years on www.speedlimit.org.uk/petrolprices.html

What are the causes of inflation?

Economists usually identify two basic causes of inflation: **demand-pull inflation** and **cost-push inflation**.

Demand-pull inflation

This is caused when the total (aggregate) demand in the economy rises. The supply of goods and services can't rise to match the increase in demand, so their prices are pulled up. This extra demand often comes from consumers, but could also come from firms (which demand capital goods for investment), consumers in foreign countries, and the government (spending more, for example, on health and social protection benefits). Demand-pull inflation often happens when the economy is near to full employment, so this is why the supply of goods and services can't rise to meet the demand.

Some economists believe demand cannot rise unless the supply of money to finance the demand rises. They would argue that this is **monetary inflation** – the money supply grows more quickly than the supply of goods and services, pulling their prices up.

Cost-push inflation

This is caused when costs of production rise and cause the price level to rise.

The main cost of production for most producers is wages. Wage costs are well over half the total costs for most producers, and in some cases much more, especially in service industries. If wages rise more quickly than productivity rises, the cost per unit of output will rise. Let us look more closely at this. Productivity is output per worker. So if each worker is paid a 2% pay rise when their productivity goes up by 2%, then the cost per unit has not risen. But if each worker gets a 5% pay rise, then costs per unit do rise (by about 3%) and are likely to be passed on in higher prices to the consumers.

One of the main aims of trade unions is to achieve pay rises for their members. The stronger the power of the trade unions to achieve pay rises, the more likely it is that cost-push inflation will take place.

Other costs could rise and have inflationary effects, including the costs of fuel, materials and components, and interest costs. If supplies are imported from abroad and their cost rises, this can lead to imported inflation.

Wage-price spiral

Whatever the initial cause of inflation, it can continue in a wage-price spiral. As the price level rises, workers and their trade unions push for wages rises. When these are given, this pushes costs up further and leads to more inflation. When pushing for wage rises, workers may take into account not just past inflation, but future inflation too. This will make the wage-price spiral worse, with higher rates of inflation.

KEY TERMS
Consumer Prices Index – the official measure of the rate of inflation.

Monetary inflation – inflation caused by growth in the economy's money supply.

Demand-pull inflation – inflation caused by excess demand in the economy.

Cost-push inflation – inflation caused by a rise in costs in the economy.

4.6 Consequences of inflation

If you have completed the activities in the previous spread, it will be fairly obvious that UK prices have risen a lot over time. Does it matter?

LEARNING OUTCOME:

The next two pages will help you to:

- analyse the benefits of price stability
- analyse the costs of inflation
- evaluate the consequences of inflation.

AO1, AO2 and AO3 skills   ACTIVITIES

What price changes are you aware of over the course of your life? Would you have preferred no price rises? How have recent price changes affected you?

What are the benefits of price stability?

We all use money to buy and sell goods and services. If the value of that money itself is changing because of inflation, it makes life more difficult for us. With price stability, we know the prices of things and can plan our spending – we know what we can and can't afford. We know that we can save our money to make a large purchase later on. Price stability overcomes all the disadvantages of inflation.

Are there any benefits of inflation?

Price stability need not mean no change at all in the price level. In the UK, we have a target of a 2% inflation rate, and a low rate such as this has certain benefits. It allows greater flexibility in a growing economy than zero inflation, as it is easier for relative prices to adjust. This is especially true of wages – the price of labour. While it is very unlikely that workers would accept a cut in wages if there was zero inflation, they might accept a rise that does not keep up with a low inflation rate.

A low rate of inflation may act as an incentive for businesses to invest as they will be able to increase their prices and profits.

Debtors are people with debts – they owe money to others. Debtors gain in times of inflation because the real value of their debt goes down. The higher the rate of inflation, the more they gain. Furthermore, if they have bought an asset such as a house with the loan, the monetary value of this asset will have risen.

What are the costs of inflation?

Inflation at anything other than a low rate will bring a number of disadvantages to an economy.

Shoe leather costs

If prices are not stable, consumers and firms spend more time 'shopping around' to find a reasonable price. This extra time and effort is known as 'shoe leather costs'.

Menu costs

Firms have to adjust their price lists more often when there is inflation, for example restaurants increasing the prices on their menus. And there are extra costs when items of capital equipment, such as vending machines, have to be changed.

Income redistribution problems

Some people (especially debtors) may gain from inflation. Workers with a strong trade union may be able to achieve wage rises that keep up with inflation. But many people may be worse off because of inflation. Those on low, fixed incomes may face hardship as their income fails to keep up with prices. This may include those who rely on state benefits for their income (although in practice the government usually index-links these, which means they are linked to the rate of inflation), and workers in low-paid occupations with weak bargaining power.

Savers are losers in times of inflation. The purchasing power of their savings falls over time, and the greater the rate of inflation, the more quickly their savings lose value. Similarly, creditors lose – when debtors repay their loans, the real value repaid is lower than when the loan was taken out.

Labour market problems

Workers will want wage rises to keep up with inflation. If inflation was 5% over the past year, the workers would need a 5% wage rise just to get back to where they were a year ago. They would need more than 5% to become any better off, and they will want to take account of expected future inflation. They may, for example, ask for a 10% pay rise. The employers, meanwhile, are facing falling sales as their costs and prices rise, and are reluctant to pay such a wage rise. This can lead to conflict between workers and employers, and there could be more labour market problems such as strikes.

Balance of payments problems

These will arise particularly when the rate of inflation is higher than the inflation rates in the countries with which we trade. As exports become more expensive because of inflation, they are less competitive and sales fall. Meanwhile, imports become more competitive against the higher-priced British goods in the UK market, and purchases of imports rise. With reduced exports and increased imports, the current account of the balance of payments becomes a larger deficit.

Unemployment

If UK producers are selling less both abroad and in the UK home market, they will need fewer workers. This will lead to unemployment. High inflation reduces the confidence of businesses and they are less likely to invest. This reduces employment opportunities in the longer run and has an adverse effect on economic growth.

The danger of hyperinflation

We have seen that once inflation starts, it is likely to continue in a wage–price spiral and become worse – the rate of inflation becomes higher and higher over time. If nothing is done to combat this, it can lead to **hyperinflation**, when the rate of inflation is so great that the currency is close to worthless as all confidence in it is lost.

> **KEY TERM**
>
> **Hyperinflation** – a rate of inflation so high that the value of money becomes close to worthless.

Evaluating the consequences of inflation

We need to weigh up the costs and benefits of inflation, and decide which are greater. We also need to consider the rate of inflation.

A very low rate of inflation may be of benefit to the economy overall. As we have seen, the UK government targets inflation at 2% per annum; it does not wish for zero inflation. It believes the benefits of a very low rate of inflation outweigh the costs.

But inflation other than at a very low rate is considered harmful to an economy. As a general rule, the higher the rate of inflation, the worse the effects on the economy. Although some individuals may benefit from the inflation, the economy as a whole, and most people in it, will suffer for the reasons given above. The costs of high inflation always outweigh any benefits. At its worst, hyperinflation can lead to an economy close to collapse. The control of inflation is a major aim of government policies. How the government attempts to achieve this aim is considered in Chapter 6.

> **TAKING IT FURTHER**
>
> UK's highest rates of inflation were in the 1970s. Find out what the inflation rate reached in the 1970s, and what some of the effects were on the UK economy and its citizens.

5. How does the UK government raise and spend money?

5.1 Government income and expenditure

In 2009/10 the UK government spent about £671 billion. This is an awful lot of money! More than £10 000 for every man, woman and child in the country. What was it spent on? Where did the government get its revenue from, in order to undertake all this spending? We will find out the answers to these questions.

(a)

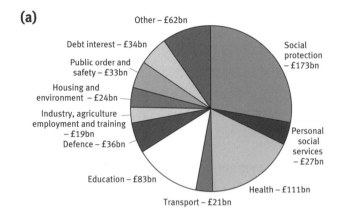

(Source: HM Treasury, *Facing global challenges: supporting people through difficult times*, Pre-Budget Report, November 2008.)

(b)

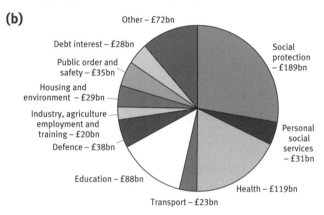

(Source: HM Treasury website, 2009. http://budget.treasury.gov.uk/where_taxpayers_money_is_spent.htm)

LEARNING OUTCOME:

The next four pages will help you to:

- identify the main areas of government expenditure
- identify the main sources of government revenue
- distinguish between direct and indirect taxes and understand their features
- explain and evaluate the economic effects of changes in direct and indirect taxes.

ACTIVITIES

Make a list of some of the services that you and your family consume, but do not have to pay for. Why are these services provided? Who does pay for them?

Government spending

The two pie charts show the projected (a) and actual (b) main areas of government spending in 2009. These include the following.

- **Social protection** – the system of social security benefits (see page 71).

- **Health** – the National Health Service provides a wide range of healthcare and protection for the population, and is a huge employer of workers.

- **Education** – most children are educated in the public (government) sector from age 4 to 16 and beyond.

- **Defence** – includes the army, air force and navy.

- **Law and order** – includes police, courts and the prison service.
- **Debt interest** – the government has borrowed money (when it had budget deficits) and has to pay interest on the outstanding loans.

Government revenue

The two pie charts show the projected (a) and actual (b) main areas of government income in 2009. Most government revenue comes from various types of **tax**. We can classify these as **direct tax** and **indirect tax**.

(a)

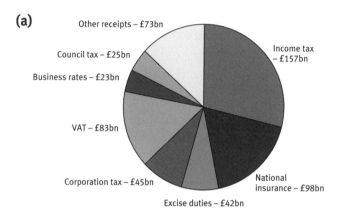

Other receipts – £73bn
Council tax – £25bn
Business rates – £23bn
VAT – £83bn
Corporation tax – £45bn
Excise duties – £42bn
National insurance – £98bn
Income tax – £157bn

(Source: HM Treasury, *Facing global challenges: supporting people through difficult times*, Pre-Budget Report, November 2008.)

(b)

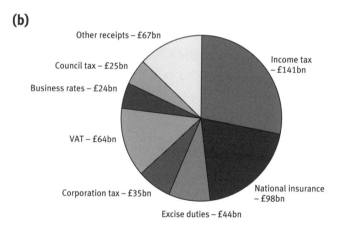

Other receipts – £67bn
Council tax – £25bn
Business rates – £24bn
VAT – £64bn
Corporation tax – £35bn
Excise duties – £44bn
National insurance – £98bn
Income tax – £141bn

(Source: HM Treasury website, 2009. http://budget.treasury.gov.uk/where_taxpayers_money_is_spent.htm)

Direct and indirect taxes

> **KEY TERMS**
>
> **Tax** – a compulsory payment to the government.
>
> **Direct tax** – a tax on income or wealth.
>
> **Indirect tax** – a tax on spending, often defined as a tax on goods and services.

Direct taxes in the UK

Income tax

This is the tax that collects more revenue than any other. It is paid by millions of people on their wages and salaries. It is also paid on other types of income, including pensions, interest, profits of non-corporate businesses and dividends. We will consider how income tax helps to redistribute incomes on page 73.

National insurance contributions (NICs)

These contributions are paid by both employees and employers. For employees, the effect is similar to income tax – a deduction from wages. Some state benefits received by individuals will depend on the national insurance contributions that those employees have made.

Corporation tax

A tax on the profits of companies.

Inheritance tax

A tax on the transfer of wealth at the time of death.

Indirect taxes in the UK

Value-added tax (VAT)

A tax on a wide range of goods and services.

The rate of VAT on most goods and services is usually 17.5%, although this has been temporarily reduced to 15%. VAT is payable, for example, on all consumer durable goods (such as TVs and mobile phones), many non-durable goods (such as crisps and chocolate), and services (such as car repairs and theme parks).

Excise duties

Taxes on a specific range of goods. In particular, there are high excise duties on tobacco products, alcoholic drinks, petrol and diesel.

Economic effects of changes in direct and indirect taxes

When the government wishes to raise extra revenue, it has a choice of whether to increase direct or indirect taxes (or some combination of the two). The choice the government makes will have certain effects on the economy, some of which we will consider here.

Direct taxes

Direct taxes help to reduce inequalities in income and make the distribution of income fairer. Indirect taxes, on the other hand, can increase inequalities and therefore be unfair to lower income groups and cause hardship for some. The effects of these taxes on income distribution are considered in more detail on pages 72–73.

Direct taxes are often said to harm incentives. Income tax, for example, which takes away part of workers' incomes, may deter those workers from working longer or seeking promotion or moving to higher-paid jobs. It could even deter people from working at all if their after tax income is not much higher than the income received from benefits when not working.

Direct taxes, including income tax and national insurance, are very noticeable when they are deducted from our pay packets. Indirect taxes, on the other hand, are usually included in the price of goods and services and so are less noticeable. And they do not have the harmful effect on effort and initiative which direct taxes may have.

Indirect taxes

An argument in favour of indirect taxes is that of choice. Taxpayers have the choice of whether or not to pay indirect taxes – they pay the tax only if they choose to purchase the commodity on which the tax is raised.

Indirect taxes will affect the pattern of demand because the level of tax is different between commodities. Consumers will usually reduce consumption of the goods and services with the highest taxes on them. Therefore the taxes are discriminating against the producers who supply those commodities. This will lead to less output and employment in those industries.

Indirect taxes can be advantageous in the case of **demerit goods** with high **external costs**. The government can put a high rate of tax on these goods so that consumers are paying towards the external costs which they cause. Motorists, for example, cause much pollution and congestion, and they are charged a high level of excise duty plus VAT on their petrol and diesel purchases. It is also argued that these high taxes will act as a deterrent so that the consumption of these demerit goods will fall.

We can see that both direct and indirect taxes have certain advantages and disadvantages. When raising extra tax revenue, the government will have to weigh up these arguments before deciding which taxes to increase.

KEY TERMS

External cost – the negative impact of an economic transaction on a party who is not directly involved in the transaction. For example, manufacturing that causes air pollution has costs for the whole population. (A negative impact is an external cost or **negative externality**; a positive impact is an external benefit or **positive externality**.)

Demerit good – a good or service whose consumption is considered unhealthy or undesirable due to its bad effects on the consumers. It is over-consumed if left to market forces. Examples include tobacco, alcohol, recreational drugs, gambling and junk food.

Demerit goods give rise to negative externalities; merit goods give rise to positive externalities.

TAKING IT FURTHER

You can use government websites such as www.statistics.gov.uk (search on 'tax') to find more details about some of the taxes named in the government revenue pie chart on page 67.

 **ACTIVITIES**

In groups, assume you are the decision-makers in government. You have already decided to spend an extra £250 million on cancer treatment within the NHS, and you need this sum in extra tax revenue. Decide from which of the following taxes you will raise the money:

- income tax
- national insurance contributions
- VAT
- excise duties
- inheritance tax
- corporation tax.

Justify your decision. Your justification can include both reasons for the chosen tax, and reasons why the other taxes were not chosen.

But high indirect taxes on goods such as cigarettes can lead to the problem of illegal activity. If taxes are higher than in other countries, then people will smuggle the goods into the country and sell them on the unofficial market. This means that the government loses out altogether on a lot of tax revenue.

5.2 Distribution and redistribution of incomes

Individuals and households have different incomes. Some people are rich, with high incomes, while others are poor and have low incomes. Why?

AO1 and AO2 skills ACTIVITIES

Think of some different occupations. Which ones would you expect to be highly paid? Are pilots and doctors paid more than cleaners and shop assistants? You can find out the pay of various occupations by looking at the job vacancies advertisements in your local paper.

Distribution of income

This is how the total income of a country is shared out among the people of the country. It is not shared out equally, so there is an uneven **distribution of income**. Some individuals and households have higher incomes than others. Why is this?

Wages

The most obvious reason is that different people have different jobs and these pay different wages. It is a general economic rule that occupations with a high demand for workers, but a relatively low supply of workers, will pay a high wage. Occupations with a low demand and a high supply will pay only a low wage. So workers in a very skilled job will tend to have a high wage, because there is a limited supply of people with those skills. This will apply to occupations such as surgeons, chartered accountants, and some lawyers. But those in unskilled jobs that most people could do tend to receive low pay, as there is a high supply of workers for these jobs. This is true of occupations such as car-park attendants, bar staff and fast-food workers. In practice, some of these jobs may pay just the national minimum wage (see page 43).

Weekly wages in selected occupations (2009)	
Occupation	**Weekly wage (£)**
Hairdresser	195
Bar worker	220
Nurse	310
Bricklayer	350
Teacher	420
Chartered accountant	675
Premier League footballer:	
Steven Gerrard	120 000
Frank Lampard	140 000
Robinho	160 000

Other incomes

Some people may have no job at all, and rely on the state for their income. This may be true of some unemployed people who receive Jobseeker's Allowance. It is also the case for a larger group of people: pensioners who rely on the state pension for their income.

Wages and salaries are by far the most important income for most households in the UK. However, there are other forms of income which some households receive. People may own assets, which earn income for their owners. Thus owners of land and property receive rent, owners of businesses or shares in companies receive profits and dividends, and people with savings receive interest. So people with a lot of assets tend to have a high income.

Redistribution of income

Redistribution happens when the government takes income from some groups and gives income to others. This is a policy of the UK government: **redistribution of income** in order to reduce **inequalities of income** between individuals and households. The way in which this is done is to take more in taxes from the higher-income groups and to give more in benefits to the lower-income groups. The taxation part of this policy is explained on pages 72–73.

There are a number of different benefits which the UK government pays to households as part of its redistribution policy. These benefits are also called **transfer payments** (as the money is transferred from taxpayers). We have already mentioned state pensions and Jobseeker's Allowance. All families receive child benefit for each child up to the age of 16. Some of you will receive Education Maintenance Allowance (EMA) if you stay in education after your GCSEs.

ACTIVITIES

'The benefits system provides practical help and financial support if you are unemployed and looking for work. It also provides you with additional income when your earnings are low, if you are bringing up children, are retired, care for someone, are ill or have a disability.'

(Source: 'Understanding the benefits system' at www.direct.gov.uk)

Use this website to find out what benefits are available.

KEY TERMS

Distribution of income – how incomes are shared out among the people of the country.

Redistribution of income – a policy to reduce the inequalities of income so that incomes are distributed more evenly.

Inequalities of income – incomes are distributed unevenly so some people have a much higher income than others.

Transfer payments – benefits to citizens which are paid out of tax revenue.

LEARNING TIP

Income and wealth are not the same.

Income is a flow of money received over time (e.g. wages). **Wealth** is a stock of assets which are owned. Wealth can earn income for the owner.

TAKING IT FURTHER

Income and wealth are unevenly spread in the UK. You can find out more by looking at the National Statistics website. Two recommended pages are:

www.statistics.gov.uk/cci/nugget.asp?id=332

www.statistics.gov.uk/cci/nugget.asp?id=2

Find out which is the less evenly distributed – income or wealth?

5.3 Taxes and redistribution of income

Taxes are not only raised to provide revenue for government spending. They also have the purpose of helping the government to redistribute incomes and reduce inequalities.

LEARNING OUTCOME:

The next two pages will help you to:
- understand the difference between progressive, proportional and regressive taxes
- identify these taxes in the UK
- understand how redistribution of income can be achieved through taxation and government spending
- evaluate the consequences of redistribution measures.

Progressive, proportional and regressive taxes

The three taxes can be illustrated as follows.

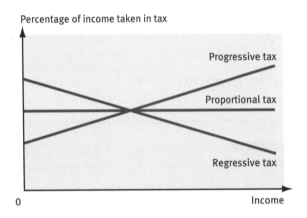

Percentage of income taken in tax

KEY TERMS

A **regressive** tax takes a greater proportion of income from lower incomes, or takes a smaller percentage of a higher income.

A **proportional** tax takes the same proportion of income from all income levels.

A **progressive** tax takes a greater proportion of income from higher incomes, or takes a smaller percentage of a lower income.

There is no argument about which option helps to redistribute incomes in favour of the lower income groups. Progressive taxes do this. By taking a larger percentage in tax from the higher-income groups, progressive taxes help to reduce inequalities.

At first glance, you might think that the UK does not have regressive taxes, but it certainly does! In fact the UK has all three of the above types of tax.

As a general rule, direct taxes tend to be proportional or progressive, and indirect taxes are regressive.

Why are indirect taxes regressive?

Excise duties are often specific, whereas VAT is set at a percentage rate, usually 17.5%. This does not mean it is a proportional tax. Assume Jay and Sarah both purchase some soft drinks, snacks and chocolate and the total VAT paid by each is £1. This £1 is a four times larger percentage of Jay's income than it is of Sarah's income. Therefore we can see that VAT is a regressive tax.

APPLY IT!

Jay earns £10 000 per year while Sarah earns £40 000 per year.

Assume the government needs to collect £10 000 tax in total from Jay and Sarah.

Option 1: Jay and Sarah each pay £5000.

This means Jay pays 50% of his income, while Sarah pays 12.5%. This is **regressive** taxation.

Option 2: Jay pays £2000 while Sarah pays £8000.

This means Jay and Sarah each pay 20% of their income. This is **proportional** taxation.

Option 3: Jay pays £1000 while Sarah pays £9000.

This means Jay pays 10% of his income while Sarah pays 22.5% of hers.

This is **progressive** taxation.

Which option is the best? Sarah might argue for option 1 as this is the best for her, but Jay would prefer option 3. A better question to ask is this: which option is fairest?

This is still a matter of opinion, although it is hard to argue that option 1 is fair.

Some indirect taxes are very regressive because they take a large percentage of a low income. This is true of excise duties on tobacco, alcoholic drinks and petrol/diesel (unless those with low incomes do not smoke, drink or drive).

In the UK, the government does not impose VAT on a range of necessities, including groceries, books and newspapers, medicines and public transport fares. This helps to reduce the regressive effects of this tax.

Why is income tax progressive?

All income tax-payers are given a tax allowance – a part of their income on which they do not have to pay tax. In 2009/10 this was £6475.

The taxable income is the total income minus the tax allowance. The taxable income is then taxed at the following rates:

- basic rate – 20% of the first £37 400 of taxable income
- higher rate – 40% of all taxable income above £37 400.

Income tax is therefore progressive for two reasons. Firstly, the tax allowance is a larger percentage of a lower income, so the tax is a lower percentage. Secondly, people on higher incomes pay a higher rate of tax on extra income. (There will also be a 50% rate from 2010.)

A summary of redistribution measures

If the government wishes to reduce inequalities in the distribution of incomes, it will increase progressive direct taxes and reduce regressive indirect taxes. It will also increase the transfer payments (benefits) paid to lower-income groups. And it can increase its own spending on measures that will help reduce inequalities. An example is providing education and training which will enable people to earn more in the future.

Evaluating the consequences of redistribution measures

Reduced inequalities

The aim of redistribution is to reduce inequalities of incomes. It can be said that the government is aiming for a fairer society. There will still be large income differences between households, but not as large as before redistribution. It also aims to ensure that each family has a basic minimum standard of living. The chart shows the effects of redistribution policies in the UK. The population is divided into fifths (quintiles). We can see that the income of the lowest quintiles is significantly boosted by the redistribution measures.

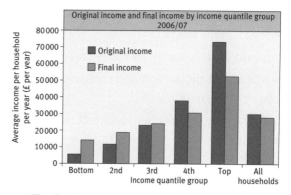

(Source: Office for National Statistics (2008) *Increase in income inequality: The effects of taxes and benefits on household income 2006/07.*)

Disincentive effects

But there will be other effects on the economy. In particular, there may be adverse effects on incentives. If people find they can live well enough on benefits provided by the government, then they may not bother to seek work – there is a disincentive to work. High progressive taxes can also act as a disincentive to work – people may decide it isn't worth the effort of doing overtime or an extra job, or going for promotion, if 40% or more of the extra income is lost in tax. Some high earners may even move abroad to escape the tax, and then the UK government loses all the revenue. High direct taxes can also act as a disincentive for businesses to invest and for individuals to save. So high progressive taxation and high state benefits which redistribute income can have adverse effects on the supply side of the economy.

5.4 Correcting market failure

In Part 1, we saw how demand and supply allocates resources according to the wishes of consumers. This is a very efficient method of allocating resources, but it does not work perfectly. If there is no government intervention in the economy, some major problems will arise – this is known as **market failure**. Here we will consider one aspect of market failure concerning externalities.

LEARNING OUTCOME:

The next two pages will help you to:

- understand what is meant by market failure
- understand that production and consumption can lead to negative externalities
- explain and evaluate policies to correct market failure, with particular regard to positive and negative externalities.

ACTIVITIES

Some of you are studying in private sector schools. Your parents are paying directly for your education. Others of you are being educated in public sector (state) schools and your family does not have to pay. Why is the state prepared to pay for this education?

What are externalities?

> **KEY TERM**
> **Market failure** – when the market (through demand and supply) fails to allocate resources in the best interests of society as a whole.

Production externalities

When production takes place, there can be effects on people in society who are not part of that production process. These people are known as third parties, and the effects are called external effects or externalities. There are often negative externalities or external costs arising from production (see pages 56–57). An example

is pollution, which could be land, air, water, visual or noise pollution. Let us assume a manufacturing business dumps its waste in the local river. This keeps its waste disposal costs down and its profits up. However, there are costs to others. People living near the river notice a horrible smell. Fishermen find dead fish floating on the surface. Local people no longer want to picnic by the river; and so on.

Consumption externalities

Consumption can also lead to negative externalities. A consumption activity which particularly leads to external costs is driving cars. This causes air and noise pollution and also creates danger for pedestrians and passengers. Thousands of people are killed or injured on UK's roads each year. Another serious negative externality from car use is congestion. Litter from consumption of snacks and fast food is another example of an external cost.

Positive externalities

There may be some external benefits from production or consumption: these are positive externalities. An example is vaccination against a contagious disease. The individual who pays to be vaccinated directly benefits because he or she is guaranteed not to catch that disease. However, they will also benefit others because they will never pass that disease on to anyone else. The vaccination is an example of a merit good.

What are government policies regarding externalities?

The government takes responsibility to correct market failure in some cases. In particular, it will try to reduce negative externalities and increase positive externalities in the economy.

Taxes and charges

One way in which the government can reduce external costs is through taxation. This is particularly the case with so-called green taxes. These are taxes that have positive effects on the environment. Excise duties and VAT on petrol are sometimes referred to as green taxes. As the increased tax puts the price up, consumption should fall, which reduces harmful emissions and congestion. The government charges vehicle excise duty on cars and other forms of road transport according to emissions, so that the most polluting cars pay a higher tax. The least polluting forms of transport have no duty at all, providing an incentive for consumers to switch to them. Other ways of making consumers pay towards the external costs which they cause include road tolls and the congestion charge.

Laws and regulation

The government may use laws to reduce or eliminate negative externalities. The government banned the use of lead in petrol, and in 2007 it banned smoking in public places. This is also known as regulation.

Subsidies

The government could encourage producers or consumers to alter their behaviour in other ways, including offering incentives to change. If the government could encourage cheap, convenient and reliable public transport, then people may use this instead of private cars, which will reduce negative externalities. One way in which the government does this is to subsidise public transport, so it is cheaper for consumers.

Provision of merit goods

The government directly provides goods and services that have positive externalities, which are known as merit goods. These include health and education services. If provision of these was left to the market, there would not be enough for the welfare of the citizens – an example of market failure. Some people would not be able to afford to pay for health and education and would be excluded from them. This would be a disadvantage not only to them, but also to third parties and to the economy as a whole. If part of the population can't access healthcare, this could lead to the spread of disease as well as a reduced workforce for the economy.

A02 skills

ACTIVITIES

Undertake a small survey among car-owning family and friends, and ask them whether the different tax bands shown in the table have made a difference to their choice of car, or might do so in the future.

TAKING IT FURTHER

The table shows how the Vehicle Excise Duty (road tax) payable is related to emissions. The higher the emissions (a demerit good), the more tax is paid.

Cars registered on or after 1 March 2001 (based on fuel type and CO_2 emissions)			
Petrol and diesel cars			
Band	**CO_2 emission (g/km)**	**12 months rate (£)**	**6 months rate (£)**
A	Up to 100	NA	NA
B	101–120	35	NA
C	121–150	120	66
D	151–165	145	79.75
E	166–185	170	93.50
F	Over 185	210	115.50
G	Over 225*	400	220
Alternative fuel car			
Band	**CO_2 emission (g/km)**	**12 months rate (£)**	**6 months rate (£)**
A	Up to 100	NA	NA
B	101–120	15	NA
C	121–150	100	55
D	151–165	125	68.75
E	166–185	150	82.50
F	Over 185	195	107.25
G	Over 225*	385	211.75
*For cars registered on or after 23/03/06. NA, Not applicable.			

Evaluating government policies regarding externalities

There are two important evaluative aspects. First – evaluate which policies will be most effective in reducing the negative externalities in a particular situation. For example, to reduce congestion on Britain's roads, would subsidies for public transport be more or less effective than road tolls? You need to consider the arguments for and against each, and draw a conclusion. You might conclude that taxing petrol is not very effective as the demand for it is price inelastic (see pages 20–21). Second – consider the wider effects of policies on individuals and/or on the whole economy. For example, more taxation on tobacco products may be justified in an attempt to reduce consumption, but it has regressive effects (see pages 72–73).

6. Which policies can the UK government use?

6.1 Fiscal policy

Can you remember the macro-economic objectives of the government which were introduced on pages 52–53? It is now time to consider the policies that can be used to try to achieve these aims. We will start with fiscal policy.

Fiscal policy can be used to affect particular markets in the economy (such as the housing market or the tobacco market) in order to achieve micro-economic objectives. But here we consider how fiscal policy is used to affect total (aggregate) demand in the economy in order to try to achieve the macro-economic objectives of the government.

LEARNING OUTCOME:

The next two pages will help you to:
- understand what is meant by fiscal policy
- understand the meaning of a balanced budget, budget surplus and budget deficit
- explain and evaluate the effects of fiscal policy.

If the government has a **balanced budget**, this has a relatively neutral effect on the economy. The government may, however, deliberately budget for either a surplus or a deficit in order to affect the economy as a whole.

How does fiscal policy work?

If the government wishes to expand or reflate the economy then it will aim for a **budget deficit**. A budget deficit aims at achieving economic growth and more employment.

If the government wishes to contract or deflate the economy then it will aim for a **budget surplus**. A budget surplus aims at reducing both inflation and a balance of payments deficit.

Reflating the economy

Let us assume that the economy is in a slowdown or recession, with high unemployment and a lack of economic growth, and that its budget is currently balanced. The government wishes to increase economic activity – to expand the economy. It can deliberately budget for a deficit. In order to achieve this, the government can spend more itself and reduce taxes.

The Budget is presented to Parliament once a year (usually in March) by the Chancellor of the Exchequer. It lays out the government's spending and tax revenue plans for the financial (fiscal) year ahead.

What is fiscal policy?

Fiscal policy is a policy that uses the government's budget to achieve its objectives (sometimes called budgetary policy).

KEY TERMS

Fiscal policy – a policy that uses taxation and government spending to try to achieve the objectives of the government.

Balanced budget – government spending is equal to tax revenue.

Budget deficit – government spending is greater than tax revenue.

Budget surplus – tax revenue is greater than government spending.

Multiplier effect – a process by which an original change in incomes in the economy leads to a total change in incomes which is a multiple of the original change.

When the government spends more itself (for example on hospitals, schools, social protection benefits), this provides income for others. As incomes rise, people are able to spend more, so consumer expenditure rises. This spending in turn provides income for firms in the economy, which will now produce more output and employ more workers to meet the extra demand. A lot of the extra incomes to firms and their workers will in turn be spent, and the process continues. This is the **multiplier effect** on the economy, with incomes, output and employment all rising. The government's extra spending leading to a budget deficit has stimulated economic activity in order to achieve more employment and economic growth.

When the government reduces taxes, this increases the disposable incomes of taxpayers. With greater disposable incomes these people are able to spend more, so consumer expenditure rises. This spending in turn provides income for firms in the economy which will now produce more output and employ more workers to meet the extra demand. The multiplier effect will continue as explained above. The reduction in taxation leading to a budget deficit has stimulated economic activity in order to achieve more employment and economic growth.

Deflating the economy

Let us now assume that the economy is 'overheating' with too much inflation and a large balance of payments deficit; and that its budget is currently balanced.

When the government spends less itself, this reduces income for others. As incomes fall, people are able to spend less so consumer expenditure falls. This reduction in spending in turn provides less income for firms in the economy, which will now produce less output and employ fewer workers to match the reduced demand. Incomes fall further and there is a multiplier-in-reverse effect on the economy, with incomes, output and employment all falling. The government's reduced spending leading to a budget surplus has reduced total demand in order to achieve lower inflation and a reduced balance of payments deficit.

When the government raises taxes, this decreases the disposable incomes of taxpayers. With less disposable incomes these people are less able to spend so consumer expenditure falls. This reduction

in spending in turn means lower incomes for firms in the economy which will now produce less output and employ fewer workers to match the reduced demand. The multiplier-in-reverse effect will continue as explained above. The rise in taxation leading to a budget surplus has reduced total demand in order to achieve lower inflation and a reduced balance of payments deficit.

ACTIVITIES

If you go to www.statistics.gov.uk/statbase, you can find out each year's budget deficit or surplus in the period since the Second World War.

Evaluating the effects of fiscal policy

Fiscal policy can certainly affect total (aggregate) demand in the economy. What is not certain is how far demand is affected. For example, if the government reduces taxes to raise disposable incomes, then people will spend more. But how much more? The government knows there will be a multiplier effect, but it does not know its value. In practice, people might save a lot of their extra disposable income or, more likely, they might spend it on imports. This reduces the multiplier effect and makes fiscal policy less effective in achieving more employment and growth.

The government will raise taxes as part of a budget surplus to combat inflation. But there is a danger that as disposable incomes fall, workers may push for wage rises which will be inflationary. The information on which the government makes its tax and spending decisions may be incomplete or out of date. Also, fiscal measures take time to put into effect, during which the economy will be changing, perhaps in ways in which the government had not anticipated. Furthermore, shocks may occur which put the policy off course, such as terrorist attacks or the doubling of world oil prices.

A final problem concerns the conflict between objectives – between trying to reduce inflation and balance of payments deficits, but increase employment and growth. This was the reason that fiscal policy became less prominent in the UK from the 1970s onwards.

6.2 Money and interest rates

Ask anyone what economics is about and they will very likely reply 'money'. But what is money?

What is money?

Money is anything that is generally acceptable in exchange for goods and services. Sellers are prepared to hand over goods and services to complete strangers in return for money. This money must be instantly recognisable to them, and they must have confidence in it, otherwise it will not perform as money. Money is a medium of exchange. It enables buying and selling to take place quickly and easily.

Imagine you lived in an economy without money – you would have to barter (swap) goods and services. That means you would have to find someone who has what you want, and who wants what you have in return. Money makes exchange quick and easy.

Money also provides a measure of value. All goods and services have a value measured in money – a price. This means you can compare prices and plan your spending. Money can also be saved – this is

sometimes called a store of value. It is also used for lending and borrowing.

What form does money take?

Different items have been used as money in different societies throughout history, including shells, spears, cattle and cigarettes.

What form does money take in the UK today? When asked this question for the first time, most students say coins and banknotes (cash). Certainly this is money, and it may finance most of the transactions of a 14-year-old. But the majority of transactions by value that take place in UK are made using money in a different form: bank deposits. Most workers are paid straight into their bank account. They then pay many of their bills, such as utilities, insurance, mortgage payments, and so on, straight out of their bank account (through methods such as direct debit).

Are cheques and bank cards money?

When shopping, many people pay by credit card, debit card or occasionally by cheque. In all these cases, no cash is involved. The money is transferred from the buyer's bank deposit to that of the seller. These cards are *not* money, they are just a means of transferring money from one person or firm to another.

Bank and building society deposits are basically 'invisible money'. The money does not take a visible form, except as figures on a piece of paper or a computer screen, but it is perfectly acceptable for buying, selling, saving, borrowing and lending.

What are interest rates?

Money can be saved, and an **interest rate** is usually paid as a reward for saving. If you save money in a bank or building society, the money does not just lie idle in a vault. The bank or building society uses your savings and those of other savers to lend to individuals and firms, who are therefore borrowing from the financial institution. They will pay a rate of interest as a price for using someone else's money.

Why are there different interest rates?

At any point of time in the economy there will be many different interest rates.

Saving versus borrowing

It is a general rule that the interest rate from saving will be lower than the interest rate on borrowing. You might save in a bank account that pays 4% interest. The bank might lend this money to a firm and charge 10%. The bank is acting as an intermediary (middleman) between savers and borrowers, and the difference between the two rates pays for its costs (staff, premises and so on) and makes it a profit.

Competition between banks and building societies

There are many different interest rates available on savings at any time. Some banks and building societies may be more generous than others. Banks are owned by shareholders who expect a dividend (their share of the profit). Building societies are owned by the people who save and borrow with them, so their interest rates may be higher for savers, and lower for borrowers. All these institutions are competing for customers, and this is another reason for different rates of interest.

Other factors affecting savings rates

Within one bank or building society, there will be various savings accounts offering different rates of interest. The rate of interest will be higher:

- the greater the minimum deposit for the account
- the longer the time that the money is tied up
- when the saver is committed to a regular saving plan

- when the saver is also committed to another type of account within the same bank.

Some institutions pay a higher interest rate on internet accounts because their operational costs are lower.

Factors affecting rates on loans

Loans also have different rates of interest. There are two important factors influencing the interest rate paid on loans.

The first is risk. The greater the risk, the higher the rate of interest. A large firm well known to the bank and with a good credit record (it has always paid back on time) will be able to get a lower interest rate than a new business start-up.

The second factor is security. The greater the security offered by the borrower, the lower the interest rate. Mortgages are loans to buy property, including houses. The house is the security against the loan, so if the borrower fails to repay, the lender can repossess the house. Mortgages tend to have relatively low interest rates. By contrast, the interest rates on credit card borrowing are three or four times higher than mortgage rates. Borrowers who can offer little or no security at all may be refused loans or exploited by 'loan sharks' who charge damaging interest rates of 100% or more.

ACTIVITIES

Go in person to a bank or building society branch and pick up leaflets, or study its website.

Make a list of the various savings accounts on offer and their interest rates. Identify the reasons why some accounts are paying more interest than others.

TAKING IT FURTHER

The quality Sunday newspapers have best-buy tables for savings and loans, including mortgages.

Try to work out where would currently be the best place to save.

All rates of interest change over time. They tend to move in line with the Bank rate of interest, which is set by the Bank of England. So if the Bank of England raises its interest rate, all other interest rates will tend to move upwards.

KEY TERMS

Monetary policy – a policy aimed at affecting the total supply of money in the economy.

Interest rate policy – the use of interest rates to try to achieve the government's economic objectives.

Bank rate – the interest rate set by the Bank of England, which affects all interest rates in the economy (also called the base rate).

What is interest rate policy?

Interest rate policy is the main feature of **monetary policy** in the UK – using changes in interest rates (which are the price of money) to affect the economy.

The Monetary Policy Committee

The major objective of interest rate policy is a low and stable rate of inflation. The UK government sets a specific target for this which is 2% inflation per annum, as measured by the Consumer Prices Index (CPI). Since 1997 it has been the responsibility of the Monetary Policy Committee

(MPC) of the Bank of England to set interest rates in order to achieve this target. The Bank of England does not have any other means to achieve the inflation target; it is by setting an appropriate **Bank rate** alone that it tries to do this. It would be impossible for the economy to have exactly 2% inflation month after month, year after year; so a band of between 1 and 3% is considered acceptable. The Bank is also required to consider other aspects of the economy when setting interest rates, including employment and economic growth. However, its primary objective is the inflation target.

The MPC meets once a month to set the Bank rate. The rate set now will affect inflation in the future, up to two years ahead. So the MPC has to forecast what the inflation rate is likely to be and adjust the Bank rate to keep it on target in the future. To do this, the MPC must consider a wide range of economic data each month, including consumer and investment expenditure, the housing market, financial markets, the labour market, various cost and price indices, the exchange rate of the pound, and international issues. The minutes of each meeting are published so it is possible for us all to see the reasons for the interest rate decision. The graph shows the Bank rate and inflation from 1997 to 2009.

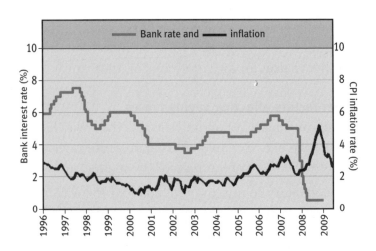

(Sources: www.bankofengland.co.uk/monetarypolicy/decisions.htm and Office for National Statistics, www.tradingeconomics.com)

How does interest rate policy work?

How do changes in interest rates affect the economy? If the MPC believes inflation is likely to rise, it will raise interest rates. This will reduce spending in the economy, so there is less pressure on prices. There are a number of reasons why total (aggregate) demand will fall.

- Saving will be more rewarding for consumers. They may save more and consume less.

- Borrowing is more expensive for consumers. In the UK, consumers finance a lot of spending through credit, especially for expensive durable goods such as cars, appliances and so on. As credit becomes more expensive, they may postpone some of this expenditure.

- Borrowing is more expensive for firms. Firms borrow to finance investment expenditure. As this becomes more expensive with higher interest rates, they cut back on their investment spending.

- Mortgage interest payments. Millions of households have a mortgage, and have to pay interest on it each month. As the monthly payments rise with an increase in interest rates, their disposable income falls. They have less money left to spend on everything else.

As well as the effects on demand, a rise in interest rates tends to raise the external value of the currency (the exchange rate goes up). This will make imports cheaper and help to reduce inflation.

Evaluating the effects of interest rate policy
Time lags

The MPC meets every month, so it is reasonably quick to respond to the economic data that it constantly collects and studies. Interest rate policy is quicker to react than fiscal policy. But it still takes time for the full impact of interest rate changes to work their way through the economy.

Exchange rate effects

Changes in interest rates can affect the exchange rate, and this can have an undesired effect on the economy. For example, a rise in interest rates to combat inflation may lead to a higher exchange rate. This in turn makes exports more expensive abroad (less competitive) and imports cheaper, with an undesirable effect on the balance of payments.

6.4 Supply-side policies

Fiscal policy and interest rate policy are used to affect total (aggregate) demand in the economy. There are also policies which the government can use to affect the total (aggregate) supply in the economy.

You take it for granted that you can read and write, but this is only because you have been educated to do so. You are still being educated, and this is increasing your value as a future productive member of society! This education can be called a **supply-side** factor in the economy.

What is meant by supply-side policies?

KEY TERM

Supply-side policies – policies that increase the ability of the economy to supply more goods and services.

When total (aggregate) demand in the economy is equal to total (aggregate) supply, there is an equilibrium level of output (GDP). If total demand then rises further but the economy is not able to supply any more output, then real GDP will not increase, but the price level will rise; in other words, the increased demand will lead to inflation. Supply-side policies are aimed at helping the economy produce more output. If successful, this means that when demand rises in the economy, this will lead to a greater GDP without inflation being a problem.

What are the supply-side policies and how do they work?

Education and training

One of the economy's most important resources is its supply of labour. It is not just the quantity of labour that affects an economy's ability to produce, but also the quality of that labour. A well educated and trained workforce is able to produce more goods and services – it is more productive. Supply-side policies include those that encourage education and training.

The UK government does this in various ways. The number of university places has been greatly expanded, and more workers have qualifications at degree level. Students have been encouraged to stay in education beyond the age of 16; the introduction of Education Maintenance Allowance (EMA) was one method used. It introduced new Diploma courses into schools and colleges in 2008. The government also finances training bodies which provide vocational skills, especially for young people.

It can be argued that some healthcare spending also contributes to a more productive workforce.

AO2 skills ACTIVITIES

Education and training make an individual more productive and therefore increase their earning power. There is a large difference between the lifetime earnings of an average person who has only school-level qualifications and those of an average person with a degree. Do some research to find out how much more you would expect to earn with a degree. (The extra earnings will depend upon the subject specialism of the degree qualification.)

Reducing direct taxes

High direct taxation can have adverse effects on incentives. So a cut in income tax or national insurance contributions may increase the incentive to work.

It is important to realise that direct taxation can affect the incentive of low-income earners. When low-income workers receive a rise in pay (perhaps by changing jobs or working more hours), their net income may not rise very much. This is because they pay more income tax and national insurance and lose certain benefits. (This is known as the poverty trap.)

Direct taxes can also affect the incentive for firms to invest. If corporation tax on profits is too high, they may be unwilling to take the risks of investment.

The government may decide to reduce direct taxation to increase the incentives to work and invest, and thus enable the economy to increase its supply of goods and services.

Reducing benefits

People may lose the incentive to work if they can receive a similar net income from social security benefits as from working. If the system of benefits is too generous, it discourages work. A supply-side measure to help the economy would be to cut benefits. The government recently announced that it was changing the rules for Incapacity Benefit, as it is widely believed that many people receiving it are quite capable of working.

Encouraging enterprise

New businesses can benefit from a variety of tax allowances and reliefs which could cut their tax bill. These include capital allowances for investment in equipment and premises, and tax relief and credits for spending on research and development (R&D). New businesses are potentially an important part of future output and employment.

TAKING IT FURTHER

The marginal rate of income tax is the rate of tax on each extra pound which is earned.

In the UK, the highest rate of income tax in 2009/10 was 40%, but there was a time (in the 1970s) when it was as high as 83%. In fact, for some people it was 98% when unearned income was also taken into account. How likely is it that you would do extra work if you knew you would only receive 17%, or maybe only 2%, of what you have earned?

Encouraging new technology and innovation

The government has introduced a number of capital allowances schemes to encourage investment and R&D into new technology. This will help to increase the productive capacity of the economy.

Reducing monopoly power

Monopolies tend to restrict output and increase prices. Reducing monopoly power helps increase total supply in the economy. The government can control monopoly power in a number of ways. It can prohibit mergers that would lead to greater monopoly power, and force monopolies to sell off part of their operation.

Trade unions act as monopolies in labour markets. The government has in the past (especially in the 1980s) reduced the power of trade unions in a number of ways in order to improve the supply side of the economy.

Evaluating the effects of supply-side policies

Supply-side policies can target particular markets or parts of the economy in order to improve efficiency. The main problem with these policies is that they can take a long time to put into effect. Another problem is that some of the policies may face resistance from groups within the economy. A policy of reducing social protection benefits will be opposed by those who believe that it would hurt the most vulnerable in society. Trade unions will oppose policies to limit their powers. Some policies may not have the intended effects; for example a cut in income tax to increase incentives could lead people to work less because they can have the same disposable income through working fewer hours.

Increasing total supply over time enables total demand to rise and lead to more employment and growth without inflation becoming a problem. A higher quality of resources should also make UK firms more competitive, and so help achieve a balance between exports and imports. In the long run, supply-side policies can certainly help the government to achieve its economic objectives. Supply-side policies can complement interest rate policy (see pages 80–81), which is used in the shorter term to manage total (aggregate) demand.

6.5 Government policies and conflicts

We have found out that the government has three main policies with which to achieve its macro-economic objectives. We will compare these policies and consider the conflicts that can arise between policy objectives.

LEARNING OUTCOME:

The next two pages will help you to:

- compare fiscal, monetary and supply-side policies
- understand that policies to achieve one objective might have adverse effects on other policy objectives.

FOR DEBATE

Have a discussion in class about the policies currently being operated by the UK government. What is it doing with regard to fiscal, interest rate and supply-side policies? Are there any problems arising?

Comparing policies

As we have seen, fiscal and interest rate policy affect the total or aggregate demand in the economy, whereas the economy's ability to supply is affected by supply-side policies.

None of these policies will have an instant effect on the objective it is trying to achieve. But supply-side policies are likely to be more long term than fiscal and interest rate policies. Aggregate demand can be affected fairly quickly by a rise in government spending in fiscal policy and a fall in interest rates, whereas supply-side policies, such as education and training, can take a number of years to be effective.

Most changes in the government's fiscal planning are made annually in the Budget. This affects the total level of spending and taxation for fiscal policy, and the details of spending and tax measures can affect the supply side of the economy. Thus it can be said that fiscal policy and supply-side policies are not flexible enough to react to changes in the economy in the short run. The Bank of England,

however, does meet every month to set interest rates, so this policy at least is more flexible.

The government can choose its priorities when putting its fiscal and supply-side policies into practice. But the Bank of England has to place price stability at the heart of its interest rate policy – first and foremost, it must set interest rates to achieve the inflation target. Interest rate policy may therefore be less effective in achieving the other objectives of government.

Matching policies to objectives

We have seen that the government's objectives for the whole economy are to maintain full employment, achieve economic growth, achieve price stability, and achieve a balance between exports and imports. The following table summarises the policies required in order to achieve these aims.

Objective	Fiscal policy	Interest rate policy	Supply-side policies
Reducing unemployment	Budget deficit	Reduce interest rates	Policies to increase output
Achieving economic growth	Budget deficit	Reduce interest rates	Policies to increase output
Reducing inflation	Budget surplus	Raise interest rates	Policies to increase output
Reducing a balance of payments deficit	Budget surplus	Raise interest rates	Policies to increase output

We can see from this table that the four objectives do not require the same operation of fiscal and interest rate policy. This leads to possible policy conflicts.

Meanwhile, the Bank of England will be setting high interest rates to reduce demand to combat inflation. This is likely to lead to yet more unemployment. We can see that there is what economists call a **trade-off** between unemployment and inflation. In order to achieve less inflation there is more unemployment, or *vice versa*.

What would happen if interest rates were raised to control inflation, but the government had a budget deficit to reduce unemployment? The two policies would conflict and effectively cancel each other out. This would not be coordinated policy – it would be mismanagement of the economy!

ACTIVITIES

Find out the current direction of fiscal and monetary policies. For example, if there is a budget deficit, is it rising or falling? Are interest rates going up or down this year? Do you think the two policies are complementing or conflicting with each other?

LEARNING TIP

Many students get mixed up between the government's budget and the balance of payments. This is because they both have surpluses and deficits. Make sure you are not one of those confused students. See Common Mistakes, page 86.

Policy conflicts

Wouldn't it be nice if the economy could always have a healthy rate of economic growth, near to full employment, price stability, and a long-run balance between exports and imports? In practice, the government may be able to achieve some of its objectives for some of the time, but is unlikely to achieve all of the objectives all of the time! There may be conflicts between objectives when policy measures are taken.

The problem of a trade-off

Assume the economy is suffering from both unemployment and inflation. The government should adopt a budget surplus to reduce aggregate demand in order to reduce inflation. But this fall in demand is likely to make unemployment worse.

Supply-side measures could also conflict with demand-side fiscal policy. Cuts in direct taxes to increase incentives, and more spending on education and training in order to help employment, would conflict with the need for a budget surplus to combat inflation.

It is up to the government to set priorities. For example, it may decide that the short-run priority is to reduce inflation, and operate its policies towards this objective. It may further argue that once low inflation is achieved, this will help the economy to achieve more employment and growth in the long run.

TAKING IT FURTHER

In groups, collect data showing the latest trends for economic growth, unemployment, inflation and the balance of payments (exports–imports).

Put yourself in the place of government decision-makers. Which decisions would you make regarding fiscal, interest rate and supply-side policies in order to steer the economy in the right direction?

Welcome to the Exam Café for Part 2

Revision

So now you have done all the work towards the exam, it's revision time. In the next few pages, we are going to look at what you should revise, and some good ways of getting the information to stick. If you approach your revision logically and in a focused way there will be no need to panic and you will not be surprised or fazed by what you see in the exam.

Then, you need to know how you are going to be examined (page 89), and you will look at some examples of the sort of questions you might be asked and how you should answer them to get the best mark (pages 89–91). There are also sample exam questions on page 92.

REVISION TIP

Laura says:

Ask your teacher if you can play a game of 'Taboo' in class. The teacher prepares key terms on cards (such as 'progressive tax' or 'structural unemployment'). Each student takes it in turn to pick a card and explains the key term to the class – but it is taboo to say a word that is on the card. The first student to correctly identify the term wins the card.

The class can be split into two teams, so the winning team is the one with the most cards at the end of the game. Our games usually have ten cards, and we play in class at regular intervals. It definitely helps us become more familiar with the economic terms we need to know for our GCSE.

Common mistakes

Look at how many marks are allocated to each part of each question. If you write a longer answer to a two-mark question than you write for a six-mark question, then something is obviously wrong! You must allocate your valuable time in the exam room so it is not wasted on unnecessarily long answers to low-mark questions.

Common mistakes

Don't get confused between causes and effects.

- **Causes** are those factors that make something happen, for example the causes of inflation.
- **Effects** are what happens as a result, for example the effects of inflation. The effects may also be called the **consequences**.

Consider the question very carefully before starting your answer – is it asking for causes or consequences?

REVISION TIP

Talia says:

Our teacher asked us to write some 'Who Wants to be a Millionaire'-style questions for homework, based on the Economics course. Each question has four answers, only one of which is correct. We chose the value of each question – between £100 and £1 million. Our teacher then collated the questions and we played the game in class. This was a good way of getting more familiar with the content – and good fun, we all got quite competitive.

Common mistakes

1 '*A regressive tax takes a larger amount from a lower income.*' This is wrong!

A regressive tax takes a larger **proportion** (or **percentage**) from a lower income. Sarah earns £40 000 and pays £10 000 tax. Jay earns £10 000 and pays £3000 tax. Jay pays a smaller amount but a larger percentage (Sarah 25%, Jay 30%), so the tax is regressive.

Similarly, '*a progressive tax takes a higher amount from a higher income*' is not a definition.

We can see in the example above that a regressive tax can also do this. A progressive tax, by definition, takes a greater **proportion** (or **percentage**) from a higher income.

2 '*A budget deficit means that imports are greater than exports.*' This is wrong!

A budget deficit means that government spending is greater than tax revenue. It is a **balance of payments** deficit which means the value of imports is greater than the value of exports.

Similarly, do not get confused between the budget surplus and the balance of payments surplus.

3 '*A fall in the rate of inflation means that prices are falling.*' This is wrong!

The fall in the inflation rate means that prices are still **rising**, but at a **slower rate** than previously. For example, if the inflation rate falls from 4 to 2% per annum, this means the price level is now rising by 2% a year – the rate of inflation has fallen, but the general price level is still rising.

REVISION CHECKLIST – Part 2

● Not confident
● Needs more revision
○ Confident

	●	●	○
What are the economic objectives of a government?			
Objectives of government policies			
Understand the objectives of government policies, i.e. maintaining full employment, ensuring price stability, achieving high economic growth and balancing exports and imports.			
Understand that a combination of policies can be used to achieve an objective.			
Economic growth			
Understand what is meant by economic growth.			
Show how economic growth can be measured with reference to GDP.			
Distinguish between GDP and GDP per capita.			
Identify, explain and evaluate the causes of economic growth.			
Identify, explain and evaluate the costs and benefits of economic growth.			
Identify, explain and evaluate policies that a government can use to achieve economic growth.			
Employment and unemployment			
Understand what is meant by employment and unemployment.			
Explain how unemployment can be measured.			
Identify the types of unemployment and explain the causes of these.			
Explain and evaluate the consequences of unemployment.			
Explain and evaluate policies that a government can use to reduce unemployment.			
Price stability and inflation			
Understand what is meant by price stability, inflation and the rate of inflation.			
Understand how the rate of inflation can be measured with regard to the Consumer Prices Index (CPI).			
Identify and explain the causes of inflation, including cost-push and demand-pull inflation.			
Evaluate the consequences of inflation, including the costs of inflation and the benefits of price stability/a low rate of inflation.			
Explain and evaluate policies that a government can use to control inflation and achieve price stability.			
How does the UK government raise and spend its money?			
Government income and expenditure			
Identify the main areas of UK government spending.			
Identify the main sources of UK government revenue.			
Distinguish between direct and indirect taxes.			
Understand the features of direct and indirect taxes, and explain and evaluate the economic effects of changes in direct and indirect taxes.			
Redistribution of income			
Understand what is meant by the distribution and redistribution of income.			
Understand why income and wealth is unevenly distributed.			
Understand the difference between progressive, proportional and regressive taxes.			
Explain how redistribution of income and wealth can be achieved through taxation and government spending, including transfer payments.			
Evaluate the consequences of redistribution measures.			
Correcting market failure			
Understand that production and consumption can lead to negative externalities, including pollution and congestion.			
Explain and evaluate policies to correct market failure, with particular regard to positive and negative externalities.			
Which policies can the UK government use?			
Fiscal policy			
Understand what is meant by fiscal policy.			
Understand how a government can achieve a balanced budget, a budget surplus or a budget deficit.			
Explain and evaluate the effects of fiscal policy on the economy.			

continued

ExamCafé

		●	●	○
● Not confident ● Needs more revision ○ Confident				
Monetary and interest rate policy				
Understand what is meant by money and interest rates.				
Understand that there are many different rates of interest.				
Understand the reasons why there are different rates of interest.				
Understand what is meant by interest rate policy.				
Understand how interest rate policy works to achieve a target rate of inflation.				
Explain and evaluate the effects of interest rate policy on an economy.				
Supply-side policies				
Understand what is meant by supply-side policies.				
Give examples of supply-side policies and explain how they work.				
Explain and evaluate the effects of supply-side policies on the economy.				
Government policies and conflicts				
Compare fiscal, monetary and supply-side policies.				
Understand that measures to achieve one policy objective might have adverse effects on other policy objectives.				

REVISION MATRIX

Copy out and complete this revision matrix.

Question	Economic growth	Unemployment	Inflation
How is it defined?			
How is it measured?		Two measures: Claimant Count and Labour Force Survey	
What are the causes?			
What are the consequences?			
What is the government's objective?			Price stability – 2% target rate of inflation
What policies are used to achieve the objective?	Supply-side policies with fiscal and interest rate policies to stimulate demand		

Exam Preparation

This will be a paper-based exam and will be one hour in length. It will consist of three questions, each worth 20 marks. The 20 marks for each question will be broken down into four parts (a to d) worth 2, 4, 6 and 8 marks (or similar). Each of the three questions will be preceded by a piece of data, which could, for example, be a line graph, a pie diagram or a short piece of text. All questions in this paper will be compulsory. This exam will be worth 25% of your total GCSE Economics mark.

Understanding exam language

It is vital to interpret the questions correctly in the exam room. Part of this process is to look at the **command words** used in the question. These can include 'what is meant by', 'explain' and 'discuss', as shown in the example below.

What is meant by inflation? *(2 marks)*

Here an accurate **definition** is required, such as 'a persistent rise in the general price level over time'. An answer such as 'a rise in prices' is not incorrect, but it is not very specific. It is likely to achieve just one of the two marks.

Explain how inflation is measured. *(4 marks)*

The command word is '**explain**'. You need to identify what is used to measure inflation – the Consumer Prices Index – and explain how it works. As the question is for four marks, too much detail is not required.

Explain two causes of inflation. *(6 marks)*

Again the command word is '**explain**'. Here **two** causes are specified. If you write about three causes, the examiner would only award marks based on the best two explanations, with no marks for the other.

You would gain two marks for identifying the two causes (such as demand-pull and cost-push) and the rest of the marks would depend on the quality of your explanations.

Sample question 1

Discuss how the government could try to reduce the rate of inflation. *(8 marks)*

Frances's answer

The government could use fiscal, interest rate and supply-side policies to try to reduce the inflation rate.

The government's fiscal policy will have a budget surplus. This is when tax revenue is greater than government spending. This will reduce total demand in the economy and so there will be less pressure on prices.

The Bank of England raises interest rates. This too will reduce demand in the economy because it will be more expensive to borrow and people with mortgages will have less to spend after they have paid the mortgage interest.

Examiner says: a good introduction which immediately identifies the relevant policies.

Examiner says: this identifies and explains the budget surplus and briefly explains how it reduces inflation.

Examiner says: this states that interest rates have to rise, and gives reasons why total demand will fall.

Exam Café

Frances's answer continued

Examiner says: a brief but accurate summary of supply-side policies.

Supply-side policies help the economy to produce more goods and services. If output rises when demand rises, then prices do not have to rise. These policies include education, training and encouraging new technology.

Examiner says: in this paragraph we have evaluation. We are told that the policies can work together to achieve the objective of lower inflation, but there are some possible drawbacks as well.
Overall, Frances has written an excellent answer.

Overall, the government could use a combination of the three policies. Fiscal and interest rate policies will help to reduce demand in the short run, while supply-side policies will help to increase supply in the long run. However, none of these policies will work immediately and it may take some time before the rate of inflation is reduced. There is also the danger that in using these policies to reduce inflation, some other government objectives (such as more employment) may not be met.

Sample question 2

The pie diagram shows UK government taxation for the year 2008/09.

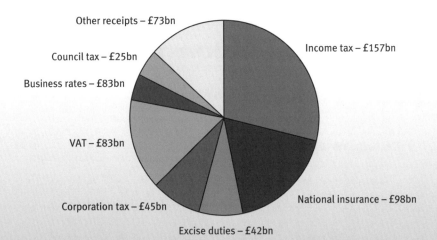

a) From the pie diagram, name the two taxes that collect the most revenue for the UK government. *(2 marks)*

b) In recent years, the UK government has been spending more on health and education. Should the extra revenue for this come from direct taxes (such as income tax) or indirect taxes (such as VAT and excise duties)? Give reasons for your answer. *(6 marks)*

Raj's answer

a) Income tax; VAT.

b) If the extra funds are taken from people's incomes, I think this would make many people unhappy with this as a large chunk of income is already taken away. But you could say that as everyone uses education and health services then everyone should pay towards them, so direct taxes should be used.

If the money were taken from VAT and excise duties it could be effective. Goods such as tobacco and alcohol are very damaging to people's health. A lot of money is spent on the health service helping people to recover from tobacco and alcohol related problems, so it is only fair that they should pay money towards it. In conclusion, I think that it would be better if the extra revenue was found from indirect taxes as this can achieve larger revenue and people are paying towards their own health.

Nina's answer

a) Income tax; National insurance.

b) I think that the extra revenue should come from direct taxes such as income tax as these tend to be progressive taxes, taking a larger percentage of the income of the higher income earners. This can be considered to be fair and will help with the redistribution of income which is an aim of the government. However, people may be less willing to work if there are high taxes on their income.

Indirect taxes seem to act regressively as they take a larger proportion of income from the poor, which I think is unfair. However, taxing goods such as alcohol and tobacco to help pay for health costs would help make the consumer pay for the external costs they cause. It also increases the price of these goods and may reduce consumption which is what the government wants to achieve to make a healthier society.

Therefore I now think that the extra revenue should come from indirect taxes on demerit goods so the consumers are paying towards the costs which these goods impose on society.

Examiner says: The two largest taxes in terms of revenue are income tax and national insurance. Raj has not recognised national insurance as a tax and has named VAT instead.

Examiner says: Raj has attempted to give both an advantage and disadvantage of using direct taxes, although he has not attempted any drawbacks of indirect taxes. There are a number of problems with Raj's answer. People probably will be unhappy paying more tax out of their incomes, but this does not reflect economic understanding. It is a mistake to assume that everyone will contribute to education and health through direct taxes, as many people do not in fact pay these (including the vast majority of students). Also, not all use the education and health services provided, as they may use the private sector instead. There is no particular reason why there should be a link between tax contributions and services used, but it is valid to argue for such a link. Raj argues that those who consume what we call demerit goods should pay a high tax, as money is required to pay for the consequences to health.

The final statement that more revenue can come from indirect taxes is incorrect. In the context of the question, the government can change any taxes to raise the given amount of extra revenue.

Overall, Raj will gain some marks but this is not a good answer.

Examiner says: Nina has changed her mind during the answer, switching from proposing direct taxes to indirect taxes! Nevertheless, this is an excellent answer. She could have used the term 'disincentive' in the final sentence of the first paragraph, but elsewhere Nina has not only used economic terms, she has explained them correctly or otherwise shown she understands them. These terms include progressive and regressive taxes, redistribution of income, external costs and demerit goods. Nina has given arguments both for and against both types of tax, and reached an overall conclusion. This is the type of evaluative answer which will achieve full marks.

Sample exam questions (Part 2)

PEUGEOT CLOSES COVENTRY FACTORY

The French car company Peugeot has closed its factory in the West Midlands. Peugeot said that this was because the Coventry factory was no longer competitive and that it would be cheaper to increase car production in eastern Europe.

About 2300 jobs were lost at the Coventry factory and another 1500 jobs lost at suppliers and in the local economy. The Peugeot closure followed closures of other car factories in the West Midlands, including MG Rover and Jaguar.

1 (a) State **two** reasons given by Peugeot for the closure of the Coventry factory. (2)

   (b) The descriptions in the following table relate to four types of unemployment. Using the words below, match each type of unemployment with its description. Write your answers in the table.

   Cyclical   **Structural**

   Technological   **Voluntary**

Description	Type of unemployment
Unemployment caused by the permanent closure of car factories	
Unemployment caused by machines taking the place of labour	
Unemployment caused by lack of demand in a recession	
Unemployment caused by people who prefer to rely on state benefits for their income	

   (4)

   (c) Would the closure of the Peugeot factory in Coventry lead to problems for the local community? Give reasons for your answer. (6)

   (d) Identify and explain **two** economic measures that the government could use to improve the employment prospects of unemployed car factory workers. Discuss how well each measure is likely to work. (8)

2 The table shows the UK rate of inflation (as measured by the Consumer Prices Index) between 2000 and 2008.

Year	Rate of inflation (% per year)
2000	2.1
2001	2.3
2002	2.2
2003	2.1
2004	2.1
2005	2.2
2006	2.2
2007	2.1
2008	3.3
(Source: Bank of England.)	

   (a) Explain what is meant by inflation (2)

   (b) (i) Explain what happened to the price level between 2001 and 2003. (2)

        (ii) Would people on a low fixed income be pleased with this change? Justify your answer. (2)

   (c) Explain how a rise in interest rates may help to control the rate of inflation in the future. (6)

   (d) Is inflation always bad for an economy? Give reasons for your answer. (8)

3 The table shows the price of 20 cigarettes in five countries of the European Union for July 2008. The tax burden is the part of the price that is made up of taxes.

Country	Price of 20 cigarettes (£)	Tax burden (£)
UK	5.66	4.33
France	4.19	3.37
Italy	2.77	2.08
Spain	1.90	1.47
Poland	1.38	1.20

   (a) Circle the two taxes on cigarettes in the UK:

   Council tax   **Excise duties**

   National insurance   **VAT** (2)

   (b) Explain why the tax on cigarettes is:

        (i) an indirect tax (2)

        (ii) a regressive tax. (2)

   (c) Explain how taxes and government spending can be used to reduce inequalities of income in the UK. (6)

   (d) Do you think the UK government is justified in putting high taxation on cigarettes? Give reasons for your answer. (8)

Answers and mark schemes are available online, go to www.heinemann.co.uk

Part 3 The UK economy and globalisation

Trade has always been a means of acquiring goods which a country does not possess. This was the way in which many animals and plants moved from their original homes to colonise large areas of the world.

Trade has always been important for the UK's economy. For example, the large parish churches in East Anglia were built on the proceeds of the wool trade. The British Empire was a large trading area, with raw materials and goods not found in the UK being exchanged for manufactured products.

Globalisation is a logical outcome of this historical trend.

When you purchase a good or service, which country did it come from? In the case of food, this is usually easy to decide, as the country of origin tells you where it was grown. But for manufactured goods and services it can be quite complex. Many goods are produced from individual components made in many different countries. Cars are a good example of this. Just because a car isn't made in the UK, it doesn't mean it has no UK parts. And when an airline wants to insure all its planes, it will need many insurers from different countries to share the risk involved.

The G8 includes eight of the largest industrialised countries: Canada, France, Germany, Italy, Japan, Russia, the UK and the USA. They meet to discuss matters of global concern. There is a move to expand the group to include countries such as China, India, Brazil and South Africa.

One way of measuring the importance of trade to a country's economy is by the ratio of trade to gross domestic product (GDP). Trade is relatively unimportant to some countries, such as the United States (with a ratio of 27.3), whereas the UK comes third out of eight (with a ratio of 57.6). When it comes to exports, the UK ranks only sixth out of eight, but for services it is second not just out of eight, but out of all the countries in the world. This is because the UK has specialised in services such as finance, banking and insurance. This is quite different from 50 or 100 years ago. In 1909, the UK's exports were based on heavy industry such as shipbuilding, iron and steel, coal and engineering.

Globalisation and trade work best when there are few or no barriers to trade. Responsibility for this lies with the World Trade Organization, which has 153 member countries representing more than 95% of world trade. Globalisation has been controversial because it has resulted in large changes in where goods are produced. This has been associated with the rise of China and India as major economic powers, and the rapid development of many other countries.

While trade and globalisation have had a variety of effects on people's standards of living, it is generally thought that they lead to economic growth, and thus to an overall rise in living standards. This can be seen by the great increase in the variety of goods and services available to the vast majority of people in the UK.

7 Why do countries trade?
7.1 Globalisation

Globalisation is not new, but it has gained in importance as countries have removed barriers to trade and as the incomes of people all over the world have increased in the period since 1960. The world has 'shrunk' in terms of what people want, where goods can be produced, and people's ability to travel to different countries.

LEARNING OUTCOME:

The next two pages will help you to:
- explain what is meant by globalisation
- evaluate the factors that have contributed to the growth of globalisation.

APPLY IT!

When you buy a sweater in the UK, the label inside may say 'made in China'. But the cotton may have come from India, the design from the USA, the dyes from Taiwan, the packaging from South Korea, and the machinery on which it was manufactured from Germany and Japan. The company making it may have started in the UK, but may now have factories not only in China, but also in India and Indonesia. The finance and insurance for the whole project may have come from the City of London.

Look at an item of clothing you have bought recently and see if you can find out where it was made, and list which other countries might have been involved.

What is globalisation?

Globalisation is an issue that arouses strong emotions in many people. There is no single agreed definition of globalisation, although it may be seen as the rapid expansion of world trade. It involves an increase in the trade in goods and services between countries. This means that countries become more interdependent and less independent.

To produce these goods and services, we have seen the emergence of very large firms that produce goods in a number of different countries and sell in a world market. These are called multinational companies. This huge increase in trade has led to an increase in the outsourcing of production, and in large sums of money moving from one country to another to finance new factories and offices.

KEY TERM
Globalisation – an expansion of world trade in goods and services leading to greater international interdependence.

One definition of globalisation, by the economist Milton Friedman, is:

'The ability to produce any good (or service) anywhere in the world, using raw materials, components, capital and technology from anywhere, sell the resulting output anywhere and place the profits anywhere.'

FOR DEBATE

Frances Cairncross, a famous economist, described globalisation as 'the death of distance'. What do you think she meant by this?

When did globalisation first start?

Globalisation is by no means a new idea. It is possible to look back and identify three major stages of globalisation.

- **Stage one** began around 1870, with an increase in international trade. New technologies helped improve transport and so reduce the costs of moving goods between countries. Stage one ended in the 1920s as countries started to protect their home industries against foreign competition – they started to restrict imports and so world trade slowed.

- **Stage two** began after 1945, when the Second World War ended. Countries were keen to build their economies again, and this led to a rapid expansion in world trade. Institutions such as the International Monetary Fund and the World Bank were founded to promote trade and economic cooperation between nations.

- **Stage three** is where we are now, and is characterised by a huge increase in trade and capital flows between countries. We also see the growth of huge companies, which need to mass-produce goods to enjoy economies of scale.

What factors have contributed to globalisation?

- **Improvements in transportation** – the costs of moving goods from one country to another by ship or plane have been reduced due to new technologies and competition. Containerisation is one of these factors, and means that goods can quickly move from ship to lorry, so handling and hence costs are reduced. With lower transport costs, goods can be traded competitively around the world.

- **Improvements in information and communication technology** – internet technology has made sending and communicating information very quick and very cheap. Contracts, orders, pictures, specifications and payments can be sent between companies and countries almost immediately at very low cost. Being able to promote products and services via the internet to a worldwide market has greatly encouraged world trade.

- **Rising real living standards** – as countries have become richer, their citizens have demanded not only more goods, but also a wider choice of products. This increase in consumer demand has greatly stimulated world trade.

- **Decline in protection** – more countries now encourage trade, so there are fewer barriers to trading. International institutions such as the World Trade Organization promote free international trade. Tariffs (taxes) placed on imports are now less common, so greater international competition and trade is possible.

- **Economies of scale** – technological improvements often mean that companies have to mass-produce and sell to large markets. This means the domestic market is not enough, and large businesses have to look overseas. Not only do they sell overseas, but often they open factories and other workplaces in other countries to take advantage of cheaper production costs, including labour. They also gain access to new markets to sell their products.

7.2 Multinationals

In the previous section we found out what is meant by globalisation, and how it has come about. An important factor in globalisation has been the growth of multinational companies.

APPLY IT!

Ford was founded, and has its headquarters, in the USA. It manufactures motor vehicles in six continents. It employs more than 87 000 people across the world. It has more than 30 factories across nine separate countries in Europe alone, and sells its motor vehicles to almost every country in the world.

Ford is a good example of a multinational company. Before you read ahead, can you name a multinational company that originated in the UK?

What is a multinational company?

A **multinational company** (MNC) is a business that has its headquarters in one country, but has operations in a range of other countries. These businesses are very large organisations. MNCs tend to be household names – as consumers, we buy from them every day.

KEY TERM
Multinational company – a company that has operations all over the world.

Examples of MNCs include Ford, Toyota, Shell, BP, Microsoft, Dell, Canon, Coca Cola and McDonald's.

Multinational corporations account for:

* 20% of production in the global economy
* 50% of the world's imports.

In addition, some MNCs have incomes larger than the gross domestic product of some countries. In 2007, the income of General Motors was larger than the gross domestic product of Austria and of Argentina.

 **ACTIVITIES**

Make a list of 10 MNCs that have not already been mentioned in this chapter. From which countries did they originally come?

Why become an MNC?

To be a successful company requires high-quality products at a low cost. Globalisation enables MNCs to achieve this by allowing them to take advantage of what different countries are best at. It would cost Sony a lot of money to manufacture televisions in Japan, but it can do so much more cheaply in China. Similarly, Unilever can make soap in England at a very high cost, but very cheaply in Thailand. MNCs can have one large manufacturing unit in one country, instead of having factories in every country. This will save money.

Advantages of MNCs

- **Gaining a strong foothold in international markets** – which is often linked with the need to gain economies of scale to remain competitive (see pages 38 and 95).

- **Cheaper labour costs** – this is very important if wages are a large part of production costs. For example, Dell Computers has recently relocated from Ireland to Poland.

- **Ability to take advantage of the different strengths of many countries** – for example, cheap labour or the availability of raw materials.

- **Transport/distribution costs** – for example, Coca-Cola has bottling and production plants all over the world, because it would be more expensive to ship products all over the world from the USA.

- **A favourable tax environment** – some countries charge lower taxes or offer tax breaks, making them more attractive to locate in.

- **Availability of government grants** – the UK government offered a grant to Nissan to set up its car factory in Sunderland, an area of high unemployment.

Countries also gain from having MNCs. They bring with them new technology while creating jobs and promoting economic growth.

TAKING IT FURTHER

Can you think of any more advantages? You might like to use the internet to search for ideas.

Disadvantages of MNCs

Due to their size, MNCs often have considerable power and influence within countries and across international markets. For this reason, they often attract criticism.

- **Loss of jobs** – when an MNC relocates to another country, jobs will be lost. This happened in the UK when Dewhirst, a clothing manufacturer which supplies Marks and Spencer, among many others, moved its manufacture of clothes to Morocco, Romania and Thailand.

- **Export of technology** – when MNCs move, not only jobs are lost, but also the technology involved in the production.

- **Dependency on imports** – although international trade means that a greater variety of products are available, it does leave a country vulnerable to closures. The UK has lost much of its manufacturing base in recent years. For example, General Motors is looking to protect American jobs by closing its loss-making Saab factory in Sweden.

- **Loss of tax revenues** – both from the MNC and from its workers. Much of the profit may go back to the parent country and thus not benefit the other countries where the MNC is operating.

TAKING IT FURTHER

Can you think of any more disadvantages? You might like to use the internet to search for ideas.

FOR DEBATE

When you have done further research, hold a debate on the role of MNCs in globalisation.

Do you think MNCs have played a positive role in world development?

7.3 International specialisation and trade

International trade has grown because countries are better at producing different products, and can gain by trading these for products that other countries are good at producing.

APPLY IT!

In the same way that we as individuals specialise in what we are best at, countries do the same.

China's main exports are: electrical and other machinery; clothing; iron and steel; optical and medical equipment.

Jamaica's main exports are: minerals; sugar; bananas; chemicals; citrus fruits; rum; coffee.

Compare these two lists. Why are they different?

What is meant by specialisation?

 **ACTIVITIES**

Look back to the work you did on specialisation (pages 10–11). Revise your knowledge and understanding of specialisation.

Compare the reasons why individuals and firms specialise with why countries specialise.

KEY TERM

Specialisation – being better than another country at providing a good or service, in terms of the quantity of output and lower cost.

Over time, countries may change the goods and services in which they specialise.

In the case of the UK, this has been because minerals have either run out (e.g. coal) or been discovered (e.g. North Sea oil). It may also be a result of a change in the costs or methods of production. Up to the 1960s, the UK was a major producer of iron and steel, ships and cars. All these fell in importance when other countries developed lower-cost and/or more efficient industries. The UK has had to expand existing areas or develop new areas of specialisation.

 **ACTIVITIES**

Use the internet to find out what are the major areas of specialisation for the UK today. Try also to find out what the UK specialised in 50 years ago, and 100 years ago.

When does a country have an absolute advantage?

KEY TERM

Absolute advantage – when a country is able to provide a good or service using fewer resources and at a lower cost than another country.

In the following example, the UK can produce more cars per person while Portugal can produce more grapes per person.

	Output per worker	
	Cars	Grapes
Portugal	5	20
UK	20	5
Total	25	25

If each country specialised in the good it was best at, we would get the following result.

	Output per worker	
	Cars	Grapes
Portugal	0	40
UK	40	0
Total	40	40

The total output of both goods has increased. This idea forms the basis of trade.

ACTIVITIES

Use your knowledge, and the internet, to decide which goods and services Jamaica and the UK would have absolute advantage in over each other. You could start by using the list of main Jamaican exports on page 98, and the information for the UK from your previous activity.

If time permits, you might like to compare the UK with other countries.

What are the benefits of international trade?

International trade brings benefits both to those who live in a country and to its firms. It:

- allows individuals and firms to obtain goods that are not available in their country – the UK can't grow many fruits, such as oranges
- increases the choice for consumers – just think of the variety of cars or food available to people, some produced in the UK, but others imported
- enables goods and services to be obtained at lower prices
- increases competition, preventing monopolies
- allows firms to gain economies of scale, increasing sales and profits
- reduces firms' reliance on domestic markets
- increases world output.

> **KEY TERM**
> **International trade** is the exchange of goods and services across international boundaries.

The growth in international trade leads to global interdependence – countries can't exist alone, but rely on each other. When economies are doing well, this will lead to greater economic growth and employment – when a recession sets in, it will spread to every country. A downturn in the economies of Western Europe and America will lead to millions of Chinese people being unemployed. This is because the goods they were making were for export, but demand has fallen.

FOR DEBATE

Do you think that the positive effects of global interdependence will generally outweigh the negative ones?

International trade and the environment

In recent years, people have realised that international trade can bring with it a variety of negative externalities.

ACTIVITIES

Look back to pages 68–69 – what is meant by negative externalities?

Before going on, try to list as many negative externalities as you can think of associated with international trade – don't forget tourism and foreign holidays. This goes beyond the pollution caused by flying to holiday destinations, there is also ecological damage to the local environment caused by too many people and the loss of local culture.

We can think of the negative externalities of international trade as being linked with the production of goods and the provision of services.

Where goods are concerned, there are three main sources of negative externalities:

- pollution from 'dirty' industries – often manufacturing is moved to countries with lower environmental standards – the higher environmental standards of countries such as the UK and USA incur higher costs
- transport of the finished goods or parts – a car may be assembled in the UK, but the parts will come from many different countries
- air miles – the majority of flowers found in supermarkets in winter are flown in from countries such as Ecuador and Kenya, contributing to global warming.

TAKING IT FURTHER

Try to find out where all the goods in your household's weekly shopping have come from.

What would happen if you stopped buying those from abroad?

7.4 The World Trade Organization

An important factor in the growth of international trade and globalisation has been the removal of barriers to free trade. This has been greatly helped first by the General Agreement on Tariffs and Trade (1947–94) and more recently by the World Trade Organization (WTO) from 1995 onwards.

APPLY IT!

If you go on holiday to any member country of the European Union, you can generally bring back whatever goods you want without paying taxes when you enter the UK, or checking whether it is legal to do so, or having to present lots of paperwork saying what the goods are or who they are to be used by. You have benefitted from free trade.

ACTIVITIES — AO1 and AO2 skills

What gifts have you or your family been given by friends or relatives returning from overseas trips? If you have had an overseas holiday yourself, did you bring any goods back?

What is meant by free trade?

Free trade is the opposite of protected trade. The debate between the two sides has been going on for hundreds of years. In the 1930s, countries tried to deal with a world recession by imposing barriers to trade in order to protect their home industries and employment. This made it more difficult for the world to recover, as demand for goods and services declined and people in export industries

became unemployed. But this has not stopped most countries from using some protectionist measures – see pages 104–105.

Free trade is a system in which the trading of goods and services between countries is unhindered by government-imposed restrictions – there is an absence of tariffs (import duties) and regulations intended to reduce or prevent trade between nations.

KEY TERM
Free trade – an absence of tariffs, quotas and regulations designed to reduce or prevent trade among nations.

Free trade enables people to sell their products to those who are willing to pay the highest price for them. That means the original producer is able to capture a larger proportion of the value of the product. In this sense, free trade is fair trade. This is especially important for producers in developing countries.

What are the benefits of free trade?

Halving the current average tariff rates would lead to a global increase in output of US$450 billion per year.

ACTIVITIES — AO1 and AO2 skills

Look back at the section on the benefits of international trade (page 99). How many of these benefits do you think are also benefits of free trade?

- **More choice of goods at the lowest price possible**. Goods are made where it is most efficient to do so. With no barriers, this means the money in your pocket can buy more.
- **Increased competition encourages firms to innovate** and to produce new products. That means you are able to buy goods that were unavailable to your parents when they were your age, or to buy better goods. Why do Nintendo and its competitors keep bringing out new models?

- **Exports of goods and services will increase economic growth** and provide employment. World trade has increased by an average of 7% every year since 1945. It is likely that many of you will be employed in jobs that depend in some way on international trade.

- **Encourages efficiency**, not only in the use of resources, but also in where they are used. Most aluminium is produced in places where there is abundant hydroelectric power, which is far friendlier to the environment than using gas or coal.

- **Increases world output and wealth**. Countries such as Qatar are very rich in oil, but without trade this would be of little benefit to them. Japan, on the other hand, has very few raw materials, so without trade it would be very poor.

What is the WTO?

The WTO is responsible for trying to increase free trade. It provides a set of rules so that members know what they are and are not allowed to do when it comes to trading between countries. It also settles disputes over trade between member countries. In July 2008 it had 153 members.

Free trade is advanced through a series of negotiations, called 'rounds'. The present one is called the Doha Round and started in 2001. The previous one was the Uruguay Round, which was completed in 1994 after more than seven years of talks. It led to:

- cuts in tariffs of around 40%

- cuts in agricultural subsidies allowing greater access to American and EU markets for developing countries' food exports

- an agreement to allow full access for textiles and clothing from developing countries

- extension of intellectual property rights, which was important for the developed countries.

The WTO does not always support free trade. Its rules can support keeping trade barriers, for example to protect consumers or prevent the spread of disease.

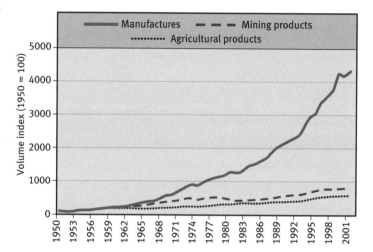

(Source: European Environment Agency, http://dataservice.eea.europa.eu/atlas/viewdata/viewpub.asp?id=1552)

The graph shows the growth in world trade from 1950 to 2001. World trade has grown 27 times in volume terms since 1950, three times faster than world output growth. While the WTO (GATT) has helped to deliver a considerable amount of trade liberalisation, progress has been uneven and success has been limited in some areas. Removing barriers to trade in agriculture and services has proved to be much more difficult than in the case of manufactured products.

7.5 Patterns of trade

Over the years there have been considerable changes in what the UK imports and exports, the countries it trades with, and the goods it trades. As you saw in the previous chapter, specialisation and trade advantages change over time.

APPLY IT!

Toyota makes cars at its factory at Burnaston near Derby. Some of the parts for the cars come from other EU countries. Some of the cars are sent to be sold in countries such as Austria and Spain.

The parts are imports because they come into the UK, while *money goes out* to pay for them.

The cars sold in Austria and Spain are exports because they go out of the UK, in return for *money coming in*.

Exports and imports

Exports consist of goods and services which UK firms provide and sell to people and firms not resident here. They result in money coming into the UK.

For example, someone from Japan flies to Manchester on British Airways. They then book into a hotel in the Lake District for a holiday. During this holiday they buy presents to take back with them to Japan. The exports are:

- the flight, which is a service provided by a UK company
- the hotel, another service provided by a UK company
- the presents, which are goods bought from UK shops.

Imports are the opposite of exports. They are goods and services provided by firms based overseas to residents of the UK. They result in money going out of the UK. If you have been on holiday abroad, think how many items you imported. Any money spent abroad or with a foreign company is an import.

ACTIVITIES
AO1 and AO2 skills

Write down five goods and five services that you have bought, both in the UK and abroad, which would be labelled imports. Which countries did they come from?

The UK's pattern of trade

The following table shows the UK's general pattern of trade in 2007, divided into goods and services. It shows that trade in goods remains more important than trade in services. Within these two sectors, the trade in manufactured goods and commercial services dominates.

UK's trade in goods and services shown as a percentage of the total		
Category	**Exports (%)**	**Imports (%)**
Goods	**59.9**	**74.5**
Agricultural products	7.6	10.7
Fuels and minerals	14.9	15.2
Manufactures	77.5	74.1
Services*	**40.1**	**25.5**
Transport	11.8	19.0
Travel	14.2	37.4
Commercial (mainly finance and business)	74.0	43.6

*Services excludes investment income and current transfers (see page 112).

Trade in both exports and imports, in the period 2000–07, has grown more quickly than real GDP.

UK's growth rate 2000–07		
	Index: 2000 = 100	**Annual growth (%)**
Real GDP	119	3
Exports by volume	134	5
Imports by volume	143	6

The UK does most of its trade with members of the EU and the USA, although China has become more important where imports are concerned. In addition to the main trading partners listed in the table below, Australia, Canada, Hong Kong and Singapore are important partners. Note that all these countries have strong historical links with the UK.

UK's main trading partners in goods			
Exports (%)		**Imports (%)**	
EU	57.4	EU	55
USA	14.7	USA	8.6
Switzerland	1.8	China	7.5
China	1.7	Norway	4.6
Japan	1.7	Japan	2.5

How has the pattern of trade changed?

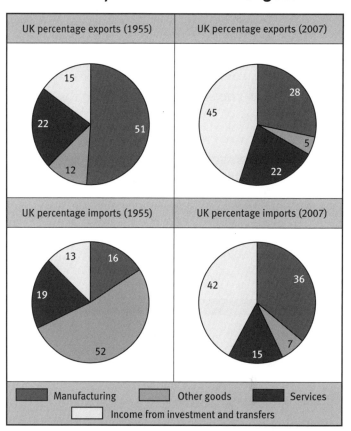

(Source: **www.statistics.gov.uk**)

As can be seen, the composition of UK trade has changed considerably, with far more emphasis on investment income and much less on goods. The composition of imports in goods has also changed, from largely raw materials to mainly manufactures.

In 1955, approximately 50% of all UK trade was with the Empire and Commonwealth. Roughly 25% was with Western Europe, 20% with the USA, and 5% with the rest of the world. Compare this with the figures above for 2007.

Countries that are growing in importance for trade with the UK include Brazil, China, India and Russia.

LEARNING TIP

Use the latest 'Pink Book' (www.statistics.gov. uk/statbase/prep/1140.asp) to find details of UK trade. Towards the end there are good charts and maps showing UK trade with the EU and other areas of the world.

7.6 Protectionism

Protectionism is the opposite of free trade. It comes about because countries may be afraid that their industries won't be able to compete with those of other countries.

Why protect some industries?

Many reasons have been put forward by countries for **protection** of their industries. Some reasons have an economic basis, while others are mainly political.

- **Infant industry**. Countries often claim that they could have a potential advantage in an industry if only they could develop it. They need to protect this industry against more efficient existing industries in other countries, so that it can grow. The question is – will it ever be possible to remove the protection?

- **Dumping**. Firms or countries may try to undercut producers by selling below the cost of production. The idea is to drive out competition, gain market share, and then raise the price to make large profits. Although illegal, this is difficult to deal with unless you can protect your industry. The EU imposed anti-dumping measures on Norwegian farmed salmon in the form of a minimum import price of €2.80 per kilogram. The EU acted in response to complaints from salmon farmers, mainly in Scotland and Ireland, that a sudden surge in imports from Norway was driving them out of business.

- **Protect jobs**. This is one of the main reasons given for protection. Only by preventing foreign goods from entering a country will unemployment be prevented.

- **Prevent negative externalities**. Countries may want to prevent goods that have negative externalities (such as illegal drugs) from entering the country. For example, when the UK had an outbreak of BSE, the French were keen to prevent the disease from spreading to France, so they banned the importing of UK meat. It then became difficult to remove the ban as French farmers had benefited from the lack of competition.

- **Political**. Countries may impose measures either to protect vital industries (for example, the US government has tried at various times to protect its steel industry), or for political policy reasons.

How may countries protect their industries?

Countries have found many different ways to protect their industries. The following are among the most commonly used.

Tariffs

A **tariff** is a tax imposed on a good or service to raise its price and reduce demand. This makes foreign imports more expensive.

ACTIVITIES

Look back to your work on the effect of tax on supply and demand (pages 30–31).

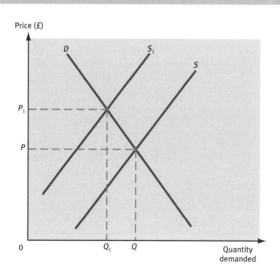

As seen in the graph above, the tax shifts the supply curve to the left, increasing the price from P to P_1 and reducing the quantity demanded from Q to Q_1.

Quota

This is a physical limit on the number of goods imported into a country. It can be in the form of a stated number (e.g. 100), or a percentage of the total market (e.g. Japanese car manufacturers are limited to 11% of the total European car market for imports from outside the EU).

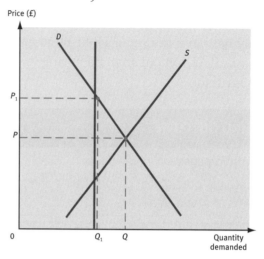

As seen in the graph above, a quota Q_1 is put into place. This reduces the quantity supplied from Q to Q_1 and raises the price from P to P_1.

Embargo

This is a ban on the import of a good or service.

Regulations

Many countries try to limit imports through a variety of rules. You may have noticed that Volvo and Saab cars which come from Sweden always have their lights on. This is because the law in Sweden requires this. All cars exported to Sweden have to change their wiring so that they obey this law, thus increasing costs. This could be seen as a very limited form of regulation.

Evaluation of protection methods

A major problem with protection is that it leads to retaliation. If one country protects an industry, then another country is likely to protect one of its industries. This is likely to result in higher prices, lower quality and less choice. The benefits of free trade are lost.

FOR DEBATE

What do you feel about the arguments for protection? Which of the arguments are strong ones, and which are not so strong?

7.7 China and India

A great change in recent years has been the growth of a number of developing countries, especially China and India. The UK has had trading relations with these countries for centuries, but until recently, except for textiles, their impact on the UK economy has been minimal. Their rapid growth has had major effects on our manufacturing industry and on our trade.

LEARNING OUTCOME:

The next two pages will help you to:

- evaluate the potential impact of China and India on patterns of world trade.

APPLY IT!

Whereas the UK managed annual economic growth of 3% in the period 2000–07, India averaged over 8% and China achieved over 10%. This growth was helped by cheap labour and other lower costs, which led to many companies in the UK and other industrialised countries moving their manufacturing to China and India. Some services, such as call centres, were also moved to India, where English is one of two official languages. Find out how many goods and services used in your household come from China and India. Ask any adults if they have used call services based in India. As a class, make a list of all these goods/services. What does this list tell us?

Trade profiles: China, India, UK			
	China	**India**	**UK**
Basic indicators			
Population (thousands, 2007)	1 319 983	1 123 319	61 034
GDP (million current US$, 2007)	3 280 053	1 170 968	2 727 806
Real GDP (2000 = 100)	197	167	119
Exports of goods and services (volume, 2000 = 100)	434	256	134
Imports of goods and services (volume, 2000 = 100)	325	302	143
Merchandise trade (2007)			
Merchandise exports, Free On Board (million US$)	1 217 776	145 325	437 807
Merchandise imports, cost insurance and freight (million US$)	955 950	216 622	619 575
Share in world total exports	8.73	1.04	3.14
Share in world total imports	6.71	1.52	4.35
Commercial services trade			
Commercial services exports (million US$)	121 655	89 746	273 002
Commercial services imports (million US$)	129 254	77 200	194 139
Share in world total exports	3.70	2.73	8.29
Share in world total imports	4.19	2.50	6.29

(Source: World Trade Organization trade profiles, http://stat.wto.org)

Compare the exports and imports of China, India and UK. Identify the differences and similarities.

How will the growth of China and India affect world trade?

Over the past ten years, China's trade has grown sevenfold, while India's has increased 3.5 times. Although both countries are having an impact, in terms of both their exports and their demand for imports (competition for food, oil and other resources), their ability to sustain this impact is not guaranteed.

At present, India has about 2% of world income and 1% of world exports. If current growth rates were maintained, India would have:

- about 4% of world income in 2025, rising to 10% in 2050
- about 3% of world exports in 2025, rising to 6% in 2050.

This means that India would still be only the twelfth largest trader in 2025, and the sixth largest in 2050. But growth depends on India being able to overcome the problem of millions of poor, illiterate people who have not benefited from, and cannot contribute to, the growth in services. One indication of India's potential difficulties is that China has been far more successful in attracting foreign direct investment.

China has to move from the manufacture of cheap goods dependent on Western industrial demand to become an economy producing goods and services that challenges the developed world. Otherwise even cheaper producers may appear.

APPLY IT!

Using the internet try to find out more about how China and India have already affected world trade.

 **ACTIVITIES**

It has been claimed that these two countries will have 65% of world trade by 2020. Discuss whether you think this is likely and what impact it would have.

Costs and benefits to UK of China's and India's growth

Benefits

- Larger markets for UK exports. UK exports to China grew by around 10% per annum in the period 2000–07. This was below that of the UK's major competitors, but if incomes continue to

increase in India and China, there will be a greater demand for services.

- Cheap imports. Prices of products such as clothes and toys were kept low by cheap imports, thus helping to control inflation and to increase real incomes.

The table below shows the areas identified in a 2009 National Audit Report as potential growth areas for UK exports to China and India.

Opportunities for UK businesses to increase trade	
To China:	**To India:**
<ul><li>advanced engineering</li><li>energy</li><li>environment and climate change</li><li>financial and professional services</li><li>ICT</li><li>infrastructure</li><li>life sciences</li></ul>	<ul><li>automotive</li><li>agribusiness</li><li>biotechnology and pharmaceuticals</li><li>civil aerospace</li><li>construction</li><li>creative and media</li><li>education, skills and leisure</li><li>engineering</li><li>environment</li><li>financial and legal services</li><li>healthcare and medical</li><li>ICT</li><li>oil and gas support services</li><li>power</li><li>transport</li><li>water</li></ul>

(Source: UK Trade & Investment: Trade Support, www.nao.org.uk/publications/0809/uk_trade__investment_trade_s.aspx)

Costs

- Loss of (mainly) manufacturing jobs as companies move production to take advantage of low labour costs.

- Potential increase in global warming as, for example, China uses cheap coal to meet its greatly increased demand for electricity.

- Rising costs of raw materials as the increase in demand from China and India outstrips growth in supply.

TAKING IT FURTHER

Produce an article for your local newspaper encouraging local businesses to consider exporting to China and India.

8 Why is the UK in the European Union?

8.1 European Union

The Treaty of Rome, which set up what has become the European Union (EU), was signed on 25 March 1957 by six countries. It has grown to include most European countries, with a membership in 2009 of 27 countries with a population of 488 million.

LEARNING OUTCOME:

The next four pages will help you to:

- identify the member countries of the EU
- explain and evaluate the advantages and disadvantages of the single market
- explain and evaluate the advantages and disadvantages of the single currency.

As you can see from the table (right), membership of the EU has increased at different times.

ACTIVITIES

- Find out which countries in Europe do not belong to the EU and why. Which countries are currently hoping to join?

Which countries belong to the EU?

EU members		
Country	**Date of membership**	**Population**
Austria	1995	8 340 924
Belgium	1957	10 666 866
Bulgaria	2007	7 640 268
Cyprus	2004	778 700
Czech Republic	2004	10 403 100
Denmark	1973	5 482 266
Estonia	2004	1 340 935
Finland	1995	5 312 415
France	1957	64 473 140
Germany	1957	82 218 000
Greece	1981	11 125 179
Hungary	2004	10 036 000
Ireland	1973	4 339 000
Italy	1957	59 619 290
Latvia	2004	2 266 000
Lithuania	2004	3 357 873
Luxembourg	1957	483 800
Malta	2004	407 810
Netherlands	1957	16 471 968
Poland	2004	38 115 641
Portugal	1986	10 599 095
Romania	2007	21 538 000
Slovakia	2004	5 400 998
Slovenia	2004	2 025 866
Spain	1986	46 063 511
Sweden	1995	9 253 675
United Kingdom	1973	61 003 875

What are the advantages of the single market?

The EU operates as a **single market** – there is free trade between members, with a common external system of tariffs (see page 100). This is called a **customs union**, and means that any firm within the EU has access to a much larger potential market.

The single market means:

- no protectionist measures on trade between member states
- elimination of border controls
- free movement of people
- mutual recognition of qualifications
- making taxes, and industrial and economic laws, the same.

Main advantages

- **Specialisation and economies of scale**. Countries can gain from the advantages of free trade, specialisation and economies of scale (see pages 95, 98 and 100). Firms can gain from the economies of selling to a market of around 500 million people.

- **Free movement of capital**. Non-EU firms are attracted to set up factories in the EU to gain access to this large market. This leads to inward investment and increased employment. The UK has gained from Japanese car firms building factories, for example at Burnaston, Swindon and Sunderland.

- **Free movement of labour**. Anyone who is a EU citizen has the right to work in any EU country. In the period 2000–07, this allowed UK firms to attract extra labour to take jobs for which there were no UK workers available.

- **Competition**. Increasing competition should improve productivity, as underperforming businesses that are not meeting consumer needs and wants will lose market share.

- **Higher economic growth and standards of living**. Ireland was one of the poorer countries in Europe when it joined; by 2007 it had the fourth highest standard of living.

KEY TERMS

Single market – the economies of different countries can be treated as one when a firm is considering its domestic market.

Customs union – a group of countries, such as the EU, have free trade between members, but a common external barrier.

Single currency – a group of countries agree to adopt the same currency and to have one monetary policy.

TAKING IT FURTHER

- Use the internet to find out the main reasons why countries might want to join the EU.

What are the disadvantages of the single market?

The single market does not mean that everyone wins.

Main disadvantages

- Increased specialisation of areas can mean **job losses**, as well as more employment in those industries. In the UK, dairy farmers have had to compete with much cheaper milk from countries such as Romania, and in many cases have had to find other ways of using the milk they produce (e.g. cheese production).

- The creation of a single market tends to **attract capital and jobs away** from the countries that are poorer and further from the population centres of the EU to countries such as France, Germany and the UK.

- At the same time, **manufacturing firms are attracted to the low labour costs** of these poorer member countries. For example, Renault has set up a factory in the Czech Republic.

- Economies of scale can allow **multinational companies to drive out local firms**, leading to these large companies gaining monopoly power and a greater uniformity of products.

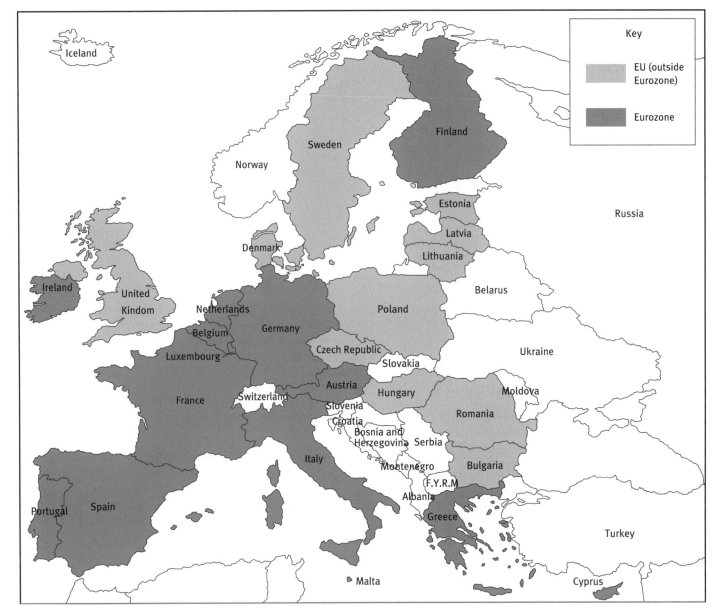

(Sources: http://europa.eu/abc/european_countries/index_en.htm and www.ecb.int/euro/intro/html/map.en.html)

FOR DEBATE

Hold a class debate on the pluses and minuses of the single market. Use the internet to obtain more information both for and against. As an evaluation exercise, write a paragraph giving a supported recommendation on whether the advantages of the single market outweigh the disadvantages.

What are the advantages of the single currency?

The **single currency**, the euro (€), was introduced on 1 January 1999, with actual notes and coins being available from 1 January 2002.

A single currency means not only the same notes and coins, but also the setting up of the European Central Bank (ECB, pictured on page 111) and with it a single monetary policy for the eurozone. The main result is that the rate of interest for the members is set by the ECB. This is like the Bank of England setting one interest rate for the whole of the UK.

Advantages

- **Elimination of exchange rate risks**. Firms buy and sell for future delivery. Having one currency removes the danger of the value changing before payment is made. This increases trade.

- **Price transparency**. It is easier to compare prices and to get the best value for money.

- **Transaction costs**. There is no need to change currencies between member countries, thus saving money. This increases trade.
- **Employment**. It is easier for people to cross into the next country to work, because their salary is paid in the same currency as they use in their own country.
- **Long-term planning**. Clearer and better information on input costs and competitors' prices enable improved opportunities for long-term planning.
- **Single monetary policy**. The ECB controls inflation across the member states by setting the rate of interest. This increases the certainty of firms when it comes to borrowing money for investment.

What are the disadvantages of the single currency?

Denmark, Sweden and the UK have refused to join the euro (the map opposite shows the members of the EU and the eurozone). The most important reason is that it gives them control over their own monetary policies and allows them to change the rate of interest to suit their needs.

Other disadvantages

- **Sensitivity to interest rates**. The nature of the UK housing market means the UK economy is sensitive to changes in the interest rate. Unlike

European countries, most UK householders own their own house and their mortgage is a high percentage of their income. UK monetary policy needs to take this into account when changing interest rates.

- **Recession**. The UK has been able to respond far more quickly than the ECB in cutting interest rates to stimulate the economy. Cutting interest rates also leads to a fall in the exchange rate, making UK exports more competitive (see pages 116–117).

FOR DEBATE

Hold a class debate on whether the UK should join the euro. As an evaluation exercise, write a paragraph giving a supported recommendation on whether or not the UK should join.

9 How is the UK's international trade recorded?

9.1 Balance of payments

The **current account** of the balance of payments concerns the UK's trade in goods and services. It deals with the UK's external trade with other countries. There is also a second part of the balance of payments, involving investment and money flows, but at this stage you only need to know about the current account.

LEARNING OUTCOME:

The next two pages will help you to:

- identify the components of the current account
- calculate the balance of trade in goods
- calculate the balance of trade in services
- calculate the current account.

What are the components of the current account?

ACTIVITIES

- Before starting this chapter, go back and revise exports and imports from pages 102–103.

The current account consists of exports of goods and services.

Goods are all those things that you could see if you were able to watch every seaport and airport, the Channel Tunnel, and the border between Northern Ireland and the Irish Republic. This is called visible trade, or the **balance of trade in goods**. Trade in goods consists of:

- manufactured goods, e.g. clothes
- semi-finished goods and components, e.g. high-carbon steel
- energy products, e.g. energy-saving light bulbs
- raw materials, e.g. iron ore
- consumer goods, e.g. fridges
- capital goods, e.g. machinery.

Services are called invisible trade because you cannot see it. The **balance of trade in services** consists of transactions such as:

- banking, insurance and consultancy services
- other financial services, including foreign exchange
- the tourism industry
- transport and shipping
- education and health services
- services associated with research and development
- the arts and culture.

Remember that exports result in money flowing *into* the UK. Imports result in money *going out of* the UK.

ACTIVITIES

- See if you can find out what goods and services are exported and imported by businesses that are local to where you live.

How do you calculate the balance of trade in goods?

UK balance of trade in goods in 2007	
	£ million
Export of goods	368 337
Import of goods	415 817
Balance of trade in goods	−47 480

This means that the UK imported more goods, by value, than it exported, so that £47 480 million flowed out of the UK.

ACTIVITIES

Before going on, do this simple calculation of the balance of trade in goods to make sure you understand how to work it out. Remember, you may be asked to do this in the exam.

Export of goods: £10 000 million
Import of goods: £ 8500 million
Balance of trade: _____

Current account – the balance of trade in goods and services plus net investment incomes from overseas assets.

Balance of trade in goods – the export of goods from the primary and secondary sectors minus the import of these goods.

Balance of trade in services – the export of tertiary sector services minus the import of these services.

How do you calculate the balance of trade in services?

This is done in a very similar way, but you may be given more information. Below is a summary of the official figures for 2007.

	Exports (£m)	Imports (£m)
Transport	16447	18636
Travel (including tourism)	18826	36158
Finance and insurance	48584	13026
Other business services	61693	34945
Government	2084	3097
Total	147634	105862

The net (difference between two figures) balance of trade in services was:

	£m
Exports	147634
Imports	105862
Balance	41772

This means that we exported more services, by value, than we imported, so that £41772 million flowed into the UK.

Using the latest 'Pink Book' (www.statistics.gov.uk/statbase/prep/1140.asp), which is the official publication of the UK's balance of payments, find out:

- in which services does the UK have a surplus (exports greater than imports)?
- in which services does the UK have a deficit (imports greater than exports)?
- can you explain why?

To decide whether a good/service is an export or an import, ask what happens to the money paid for it. Coming into the UK – export; going out of the UK – import.

AO1 and AO2 skills ACTIVITIES

Are the following exports or imports? Remember to ask yourself which way the money is going.

- Toyota sends cars from the UK to Spain.
- You buy a Nintendo® Wii™ console made in Japan.
- Aviva (UK insurance company) sells insurance policies in Germany.
- A UK pop group has a successful tour of the USA.
- You go on holiday to Portugal, flying with Ryanair.

How do you calculate the current account?

The current account is the total of all goods and services. To find this, we add the two accounts that we have already calculated together with income from investments and transfers of money. Transfers of money come about when, for example, a Hungarian waiter works in a UK hotel, but sends back money to the family in Hungary.

	Exports (£m)	Imports (£m)
Goods	368337	415817
Services	147634	105862
Income from investments and transfers	301410	306498
Total	817381	828177
Balance on current account	10796	

Calculate the current account, given the following information.

Balance of trade in goods	−£25 million
Balance of trade in services	£40 million
Income from investments and transfers	−£ 5 million

9.2 Balance of payments deficit

There has been an outflow of money on the UK's balance of payments on current account ever since 1983. This has been balanced mainly by a large inflow of investment by foreign firms wanting to set up, or expand existing, businesses in the UK.

LEARNING OUTCOME:

The next two pages will help you to:

- explain what is meant by a balance of payments deficit and surplus
- understand the reasons for a balance of payments deficit
- evaluate the methods of rectifying a balance of payments deficit.

APPLY IT!

Selina wanted to go to the Year 11 ball. She realised that the new outfit she wanted to buy cost more than her income. She would need to ask mum if she would lend her some money. It all meant that she would have to find ways of earning more money, so she could pay mum back.

Explain to Selina what is meant by a deficit.

What is meant by a balance of payments deficit and surplus?

A deficit is where your outgoings/expenditure is more than your income/revenue. In this case the value of imports exceeds that of exports, so there is an *outflow* of money.

A surplus is the exact opposite. Income/revenue is greater than outgoings/expenditure. The value of exports exceeds that of imports, so there is an *inflow* of money.

Page 113 gives a statement of the current account for 2007.

AO1 and AO2 skills
ACTIVITIES

Look back at 'How do you calculate the current account?' on page 113. Make sure you have understood the calculation and how the figure of £10 796 million was arrived at. Is this an inflow or an outflow of money?

In 2007 the UK had a deficit of £10 796 million. This means that imports were greater than exports – there was an outflow of money over the year.

What are the reasons for a balance of payments deficit?

The reasons for a deficit relate to both demand and supply factors. The factors listed below are an attempt to explain the UK's persistent deficit, but could also be applied to other countries.

- **Loss of advantage in many industries**. 100 years ago, the UK specialised in industries such as iron and steel, shipbuilding, textiles and coal mining. All of these have largely disappeared and been replaced by imports.

- **Globalisation**. With globalisation, it is cheaper to produce goods where labour costs are low. The result is that many goods that were made in the UK up to a few years ago are now made in China, India and other low-cost countries.

AO1 and AO2 skills
ACTIVITIES

Try to find out what goods were made in the area where you live 100, 50 or 25 years ago. Are they still made? If not, where are they made now?

- **Growth in people's real income**. Demand has risen more quickly than supply. To prevent a shortage of goods, the gap has been filled with imports. And as incomes rise, people want more choice, including foreign products.

- **Exchange rate**. A strong exchange rate means that the pound (sterling) buys more foreign goods, so people can afford to buy more foreign goods and services (such as foreign holidays). At the same time, UK goods are more expensive abroad, leading to a fall in demand.

- **Low levels of productivity and investment**. Compared with many of our main competitors, our labour productivity has been low, partly due to lower levels of capital investment.

- **Relatively weak product innovation**. This can be linked to a low rate of spending by businesses on research and development.

As you will have discovered earlier in the course, businesses compete both by price and quality of their goods/services. The UK will always find it very difficult to compete on price with countries such as China, because labour costs there are so much lower. And a valid criticism of the UK manufacturing industry has been that too often it fails to compete on quality.

The chart below shows the UK's **current account deficits** since 1987.

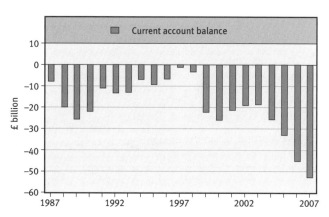

(Source: www.statistics.gov.uk/STATBASE/Product.asp?vlnk=1140)

ACTIVITIES

From a pack of cards giving a range of changes in exports and imports, each student in turn selects a card; reads it out to the group; and explains the impact it might have on the balance of payments.

How should a balance of payments deficit be dealt with?

KEY TERMS

Current account deficit – the value of imports exceeds the value of exports.

Current account surplus – the value of exports exceeds the value of imports.

FOR DEBATE

Before reading on, in pairs or groups think about the methods or policies that could be used to improve the current account deficit. You may need to refer back to previous sections.

One way of looking at this is to think about the causes of the deficit. If it is due to excess demand, then demand-side policies could be used (e.g. raising interest rates or taxes; see page 81). If UK products are being priced out of markets because the exchange rate is too high, then it may be possible to reduce the exchange rate by cutting interest rates (see page 81). These are all relatively easy to do, although it is important to be careful of the effects they may have on other areas of the economy.

ACTIVITIES

You may find it useful to revise your understanding of fiscal, monetary and supply-side policies before going on – see pages 53, 76–77 and 80–83.

Putting right the supply side takes longer, and it is more difficult to predict the outcome. Output can be improved through greater productivity and more investment. Governments can encourage this by tax incentives and through better training and education. Where inflation is high, this could be brought under control by fiscal and monetary policies so that prices are more competitive.

In theory, tariffs and other protection methods could be used, but they could lead to conflict with the WTO and the UK is bound by EU decisions on trade.

The UK's ability to compete effectively in the second decade of the twenty-first century is likely to be determined by:

- keeping inflation under control
- spending more on research and development
- improving productivity
- relying on the economic growth of our major partners, such as the EU, to provide markets for our exports.

FOR DEBATE

Evaluate the methods available to the UK for reducing its current account deficit.

10 How important is the value of a currency?

10.1 Exchange rates

The exchange rate is the rate at which one currency exchanges for another currency. Most currencies are freely exchangeable. This means I can go into any bank and buy a currency such as the euro or the US dollar for my pounds. In some cases, for example for India, I can't do that – I can only obtain Indian rupees if I actually go there.

LEARNING OUTCOME:

The next two pages will help you to:

- explain what is meant by an exchange rate
- understand and illustrate how exchange rates are determined through the interaction of demand and supply.

APPLY IT!

Terry and Joanne were going on holiday to France. They needed to take euros with them, as pounds sterling would not be accepted in most of the places they were going. Terry went to the local Post Office and exchanged pounds (£) for euros (€). When he got home, he told Joanne that he had received €496 in exchange for £400.

How many euros (€) did Terry get for each pound (£)?

What is meant by exchange rates?

The **exchange rate** between two currencies specifies how much one currency is worth in terms of the other. It is the value of a foreign nation's currency in terms of the home nation's currency.

The following graphs show the value of the pound (£) against that of the US dollar ($) and the euro (€) in late 2008/early 2009.

If £1 will buy $1.50, this means that for every £1 I can get $1.50. If I want to buy a CD released only

in the USA costing $18, then I will need to exchange £12 for it. Equally, an American visitor to the UK wanting to buy a picture priced at £500 would need to exchange $750 for it.

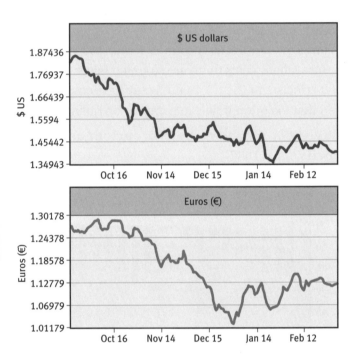

(Source: www.x-rates.com)

APPLY IT!

I have booked a hotel room in Italy for one night. The price is €120. If the exchange rate is £1 to €1.25, what is the price of the hotel room in sterling?

 **ACTIVITIES**

Using the internet, find out how the value of the pound has changed against currencies such as the US dollar, the euro and the Japanese yen (¥) since you started studying economics.

How are exchange rates determined?

Most exchange rates are determined by the market forces of supply and demand.

Exchange rates can either be decided by the market – **floating exchange rates**; or fixed by the central bank – **fixed exchange rates**. The diagram below shows a floating rate.

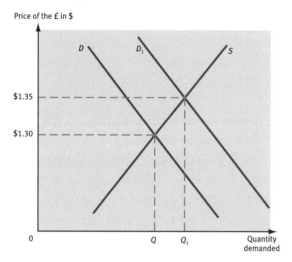

Price of the £ in $

KEY TERMS

Exchange rate – how much of one currency needs to be given up to buy one unit of another currency.

Floating exchange rate – where the prices of two currencies are decided by market forces.

Fixed exchange rate – where the central bank of a country tries to decide on the price of a currency.

Originally, the price of the pound in terms of the dollar was $1.30 – for every £1 you would get $1.30. If demand for pounds increased, for example if more Americans decided to come on holiday to the UK, then the demand curve would shift to the right, to D_1. This increases the price of a pound to $1.35.

The diagram below shows what happened in late 2008, when foreign holders of the pound lost confidence in

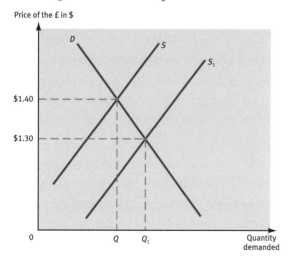

Price of the £ in $

the UK economy. More pounds were sold, leading to an increase in the supply from S to S_1. This led to a fall in the price of the pound from $1.40 to $1.30.

Some countries still try to fix their exchange rates. This is done in one of two ways.

- India, for example, does not allow its currency to be bought and sold freely. If you visit India you can't buy rupees (Indian currency) until you are in the country. The rate is fixed by the Reserve Bank of India (India's version of the Bank of England).

- China fixes its rate through the People's Bank of China buying and selling the yuan (China's currency) in the foreign exchange market so as to maintain its value at a fixed price. This can be seen in the diagram below.

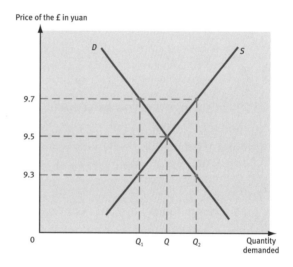

Price of the £ in yuan

In the diagram, the fixed rate is 9.5 yuan to the pound. If demand for the yuan rose so the price increased to 9.7 yuan, then the Bank would sell yuan and buy pounds, thus leading to a rise in the price of the pound and a fall in the price of the yuan. The opposite would happen if there was selling of the yuan, leading to its fall to 9.3 yuan.

TAKING IT FURTHER

Draw two diagrams to illustrate the ideas expressed above. Start from the diagram above.

Show how an increase in demand for the yuan would affect its price, and then how selling the yuan could bring the price back to its original value. Explain your diagram.

10.2 Exchange rates, the rate of interest and trade

The exchange rate, especially when determined by market forces, will be affected by changes in the rates of interest offered in different countries. Equally, the exchange rate will affect exports and imports, and how competitive a country is when trading.

APPLY IT!

If you have £100 in savings and you don't want to spend it, you look for the best rate of interest. If one bank can offer you 1% more, you will move your money to that bank. In that way you get the most interest you can.

If you went on a foreign holiday in 2007, your parents may have said how much further their money was going. The pound had risen in value, making imports cheaper. The opposite has happened in 2009, so fewer people are travelling to the USA or Europe because it is now more expensive.

Find out how much a holiday to France would have cost in 2007 and in 2009, or in any two different years. Why do you think the price has changed?

How do changes in interest rates affect exchange rates?

International holders of money operate in the same way as you and I do, except that they move money between banks in different countries as interest rates change.

As we saw on pages 116–117, movements of money in and out of a country to pay for exports and imports affect the value of the exchange rate.

 ACTIVITIES

If you are not sure about either interest rates or how the exchange rate moves, revise units 6.3 and 10.1 before reading further.

If the rate of interest in the UK goes up, this makes holding bank deposits in London more attractive. Someone in Zurich (Switzerland) might then move their money from New York to London. To do so, they would need to convert the deposit from dollars to pounds. They would do this by selling dollars and buying pounds. This would increase the demand for pounds, leading to a rise in the price of sterling.

AO1 and AO2 skills ACTIVITIES

- Draw a supply and demand diagram to show what will happen to the pound if the rate of interest in the UK goes up.
- Draw another diagram to show what might happen if the rate of interest in the UK fell.

As you have found out, in the same way as changes in the current account affect the value of the pound (page 112), so changes in the rates of interest between different countries also affect the value of the pound.

The currencies which are most often traded are the US dollar, the euro, the Japanese yen and the UK pound. This means that changes (e.g. in interest rates) in New York, Frankfurt, Tokyo and London, respectively, will have the most effect on the values of these currencies.

When the UK interest rate rose to 5.75% in July 2007, the value of the pound rose to US$2. Equally, when the interest rate fell to 0.5% in March 2009, the exchange rate fell to $1.40.

ACTIVITIES

Use the internet to find out what has happened to the rate of interest in the UK, and the current value of the exchange rate.

Why might a rise or fall in the UK interest rate not affect the exchange rate? You might wish to discuss this in small groups and then compare your ideas.

How can exchange rates affect trade and international competitiveness?

> **KEY TERM**
>
> **International competitiveness** – the ability of companies to compete with companies from other countries.

ACTIVITIES

- In pairs, try to analyse what might happen to UK exports and imports if the value of the pound rose. Why might this happen?
- Then consider how the price elasticity of demand for exports and imports might affect the outcome.

Exchange rates are an important, but not the only, factor that could affect trade.

If the value of the pound rose, this would mean that UK exports would be more expensive to buyers in other countries, while UK imports would be cheaper. This makes it difficult to sell goods and services to other countries because they can find substitutes that are cheaper. Equally, foreign companies find it easier to sell their products in the UK because they are cheaper. You can see the outcome of this in 2007 by looking at the current account deficit chart on page 115. Notice that the rising value of the pound led to an increased current account deficit.

International competitiveness is the ability of the companies in one country to compete with those in other countries. It is measured by success in selling goods and services.

Pound could soon be worth just one euro

Hugo Duncan and Sri Carmichael

Sterling was today on course for its worst week ever against the European single currency, raising the prospect of a one pound euro.

The pound traded at 87.2p per euro, meaning it has lost five per cent since opening the week at 82.7p – the largest fall since the single currency was launched in 1999.

It is down 20 per cent on a year ago.

The pound also fell 0.10 cents against the US dollar to $1.468, leaving sterling down 30 per cent from its peak of more than $2 in the summer.

It means skiers face record costs this winter on ski passes, hotels and meals in Europe and North America.

(Source: www.thisislondon.co.uk/standard)

ACTIVITIES

- In pairs, try to think of different ways in which companies from different countries could compete to sell their products. Compare your list with those of other pairs.
- You will find that, although price was probably on every list, there are many other factors affecting the ability to compete. One good example is BMW, which has competed mainly on the quality of the car, rather than its price.

Nevertheless, price is important. A fall in the value of the pound would make UK products more competitive, because the pound would be cheaper and thus the price of UK exports would fall. This would lead to more exports and fewer imports, improving the current account.

ACTIVITIES

From a pack of cards giving a range of changes in exchange rates, each student in turn selects a card; reads it out to the group; and explains the impact the change might have on, for example, exporters, importers, tourism, competitiveness, and the current account.

FOR DEBATE

You need to be able to 'explain and evaluate' the impact of changes in exchange rates on trade and international competitiveness.

Discuss in a group what you think you could write about this. Remember – you are trying to decide how important the exchange rate is for trade and for international competitiveness.

11 How does a country become more competitive?

11.1 Factors influencing competitiveness

UK businesses face competition both at home (from imports) and abroad (from other countries' exports and from the domestically produced goods and services of the importing country). While businesses can't easily influence the exchange rate, there are other ways in which they can try to remain **competitive**.

LEARNING OUTCOME:

The next two pages will help you to:

- appreciate the importance of wages and relative unit costs
- understand the importance of the exchange rate
- understand the importance of productivity
- understand the importance of other costs.

APPLY IT!

A recent study by the Chartered Management Institute identified 17 possible situations of change facing managers and organisations in the next 10 years. These range from a world run by robots, where advances in artificial intelligence gradually increase our dependence on technology systems, to an ageing workforce with different abilities and needs. All these will affect competitiveness both positively and negatively.

Try to think of four more possible changes that could occur in the next 10 years. Will these have a positive or negative effect on competitiveness?

KEY TERM

Competitiveness – the ability of a country to compete successfully internationally and maintain improvements in real output and wealth.

ACTIVITIES

In groups, identify as many factors as possible that you think could affect the ability of UK businesses to compete in the world market.

Why are wages and relative unit cost important for competitiveness?

The great advantage that countries such as China, India and some Eastern European countries have, compared with the UK, is the level of wages.

APPLY IT!

In 2003, Dyson closed its washing machine plant in the UK and moved it to Malaysia because the cost per unit was much lower, mainly due to lower wages. This allowed Dyson to remain competitive with other washing machine producers who were already manufacturing in low-wage countries. If Dyson had not moved its manufacturing, it could have found its prices undercut by rivals with lower unit costs.

Which other goods and services could benefit from low wages, and which would not be influenced by this? Your list will contain products where labour costs are a high percentage of total costs.

Wages are very important where a lot of labour is involved in the product. Washing machines require all the parts to be assembled by people, which costs money. Services such as tourism can also carry high labour costs.

Why is the exchange rate important for competitiveness?

If you are not sure about this, look back at the previous chapter.

FOR DEBATE

What effect would a rise in the external value of the pound have on the competitiveness of UK's businesses? Discuss this in pairs before reading further.

If the exchange rate rises, this means that UK exports cost more. They are *less* competitive. Imports, however, are cheaper, which would make them *more* competitive in the UK, compared with UK products.

Where UK goods use a lot of imported materials in their manufacture, costs will fall. This may make the goods cheaper to produce. The fall in the cost could then offset the rise in the exchange rate, so that competitiveness is not directly affected.

Unlike other factors, the exchange rate can immediately affect competitiveness.

ACTIVITIES

Using a newspaper or the internet, record for a week the exchange rate of the pound against the dollar and the euro. How have the changes affected the competitiveness of UK businesses?

Why is productivity important for competitiveness?

Refresh your understanding of productivity by going back to Chapter 3. Make sure you know the definition of productivity.

One way to remain competitive despite higher wages and other costs, and a rising value of your currency, is to increase productivity.

Increasing productivity means that any rise in costs is offset by greater output for each worker. In 2007 the Nissan car factory at Sunderland had the highest level of productivity of all car factories in Europe. This helped Nissan offset the high value of the pound.

As can be seen below, although the UK has improved its productivity when compared with major rivals, it is still behind the USA, for example, by nearly 20%.

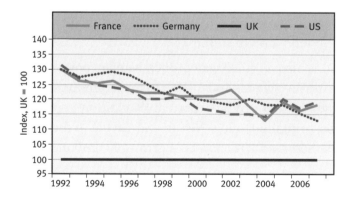

Productivity in terms of output and time worked (index, UK = 100).
(Source: Office for National Statistics: www.dtistats.net/competitiveness5)

Remember, businesses that achieve high levels of productivity can be low-cost producers while at the same time paying high wages.

ACTIVITIES

The Department for Business, Enterprise and Regulatory Reform suggests that productivity depends on investment, innovation, skills, enterprise and competition.

In groups, discuss how each of these could affect productivity and competitiveness.

What is the importance of other costs for competitiveness?

ACTIVITIES

Before reading further, write down what other possible costs might affect competitiveness. Compare your list with others around you.

From the activity you will probably have a long list. Below are three important ones.

- **Raw materials**. Countries such as the UK have to import most of their raw materials. If the price rises, this will push up the cost of production and make UK goods less competitive than those of countries that have their own sources of raw materials. This is one reason why China has been buying shares in many mining companies so as to be able to get raw materials at favourable prices.

- **Government regulation**. UK businesses often complain that excessive regulation costs them money and makes them less competitive than firms in other countries. Time spent on filling in forms and making sure all rules are complied with is time – and money – not spent on production.

- **Keeping up to date**. Making sure that:
  - all the workers maintain and improve their skills so they can use the latest equipment and are more productive; and
  - the equipment itself is up-to-date

costs money, but is essential to avoid falling behind competitors. Businesses also need to ensure the money is well spent, otherwise costs will rise.

- And if you wrote down inflation, then you have identified another important cost that will be discussed in the next chapter.

11.2 Government policy and international competitiveness

As we have seen in previous chapters, competitiveness is essential for UK business to survive. This can be helped or hindered by government policies.

LEARNING OUTCOME:

The next two pages will help you to:

- understand the importance of low inflation
- understand the importance of sustainable economic growth
- understand the importance of incentives for investment
- evaluate the importance of investment in education and training
- discuss and evaluate government policies aimed at improving UK international competitiveness.

The government is keen to improve education and training and to make sure all young people have opportunities – a better educated and trained workforce is needed if the UK is to compete.

Why is low inflation important?

 **ACTIVITIES**

What would happen in terms of UK exports and imports if inflation was 6% in the UK, but only 2% in our major trading partner? How would this affect the UK's current account? Discuss this in pairs.

The answer is that UK prices would make exports more expensive than foreign products, but imports cheaper than UK products. The UK would be less competitive – sell less abroad, but buy more foreign products. This would have a negative effect on the current account.

The UK government has been keen to keep inflation low, in line with that of our major competitors.

 **ACTIVITIES**

Use the internet to gather information on how the UK's rate of inflation has compared with that of France, Germany, Japan and the USA over a period of years.

Why is sustainable economic growth important?

If economic growth cannot be sustained, then living standards will fall, unemployment will rise and the country will lose out to competitors.

Why are incentives for investment important?

In a global economy, countries are not only trying to remain competitive, but also wish to attract **foreign direct investment** (FDI) in terms of, for example, new factories. This FDI brings with it new technology and more jobs.

KEY TERM

Foreign direct investment – the investment by foreign companies in the production of goods and services in another country.

It is estimated that in the 1990s, the UK government paid subsidies of around £15 000 to £25 000 per employee to bring Samsung and Siemens to north-east England. The intention was to introduce new industries to the area, which suffered from high levels of unemployment.

The Irish Republic, which is situated on the edge of Europe, used a range of incentives in the 1990s to make its locations more attractive than other possibilities – and achieved the highest level of economic growth in the EU.

FDI is also another way of increasing exports. Many countries give tax incentives to firms producing products that can be exported. In addition to creating jobs, bringing Honda, Nissan and Toyota to the UK has increased UK exports of cars and components.

Incentives are also needed to reduce the costs of research and development (R&D). Without sufficient R&D, inventions and innovations are less likely to be made, reducing competitiveness and economic growth.

Investment not only generates new ideas and industries, and regenerates existing industries, but positively affects other firms and the economy of the area in which the investment takes place (economists call this the multiplier effect).

ACTIVITIES

Using local newspapers and the internet, find out what investment has recently taken place where you live. What effects is this expected to have on the local economy? Has the government, or your local council, given any support for it? If so, why?

How important is investment in education and training?

ACTIVITIES

What do you think is meant by 'investment in education and training'? Write down as many examples as you can think of. Compare your list with others in your class. Why might your ideas be important?

In 2006, the European Trade Union Confederation (ETUC) stated that: 'On the European labour market there are 100 million workers who are at risk due to their level of qualifications, and 20 million unemployed. The ETUC will emphasise that enhancing their skills and qualifications is crucial for Europe's competitiveness' (www.etuc.org/a/3116).

Education and training ensure that everyone can participate in, and contribute to, an economy. Benefits are felt not only by the people who are being educated and trained (private benefit), but also by the country as a whole, for example through increased productivity (external benefit).

Without an educated and trained workforce, not only will investment in R&D not be effective, but new inventions will not be put into operation because the necessary skills will be lacking.

How effective are government policies in improving UK international competitiveness?

As seen in the table, the Centre for International Competitiveness ranking of European countries has seen an improvement for the UK between 2004 and 2007. This could be an indication that government policies have been effective.

Nation	Ranking	
	2007	2004
Finland	1	5
Luxembourg	2	2
Switzerland	3	1
Norway	4	3
Denmark	5	4
Sweden	6	6
Netherlands	7	7
United Kingdom	8	10
Austria	9	12
France	10	9
Belgium	11	11
Germany	12	8
Ireland	13	13
Italy	14	14
Spain	15	15
Slovenia	16	–
Greece	17	17
Portugal	18	16
Cyprus	19	–
Malta	20	–
Hungary	21	–
Czech Republic	22	–
Slovakia	23	–
Poland	24	–
Estonia	25	–
Lithuania	26	–
Latvia	27	–
(Source: www.cforic.org/downloads.php)		

There are many ways in which effectiveness could be measured.

- **Education and training** – are UK workers more skilled, and has their productivity increased? Evidence points to lower productivity than many of our competitors.
- **Current account** – interest rates have been targeted at inflation. As in 2007–08, this has made our exports more expensive and imports cheaper. This meant our products were less competitive.
- **Attractive to FDI** – the UK has seen the largest inflow of FDI in the EU. This points to policies that have been seen by foreign businesses as favourable for investment. This should make UK products more competitive.

ACTIVITIES

Using a newspaper or the internet, find out what FDI has taken place in your town or region. Discuss how important it has been in improving the competitiveness of business in your town/region.

11.3 The UK and globalisation

There are many arguments both for and against the view that the UK has benefited from globalisation. Some people and businesses have gained – and some have lost. What is needed is an overall evaluation.

This chapter sets out a range of arguments both for and against, some of which have been covered in previous chapters. You are then asked to reach your own conclusion.

LEARNING OUTCOME:

The next two pages will help you to:

- evaluate the extent to which globalisation has benefited the UK.

AO1 and AO2 skills ACTIVITIES

Look at the goods and services that you and your family use and own. Who has made them? Where have they come from? If they are not produced by UK firms in the UK, then think about what benefit you have had from them. Have they given you more choice? Are they cheaper, so your money goes further? Are they better quality?

Before starting this chapter, go back to the early chapters in this unit and make sure you understand the issues involved in globalisation, multinationals, specialisation, etc.

What are the benefits of globalisation to the UK?

- The following have been discussed in chapter 4:
  - low inflation due to greater competition and ability to produce in low-cost countries
  - sustained economic growth from the mid-1990s to 2008, helped by rising levels of investment and trade
  - high levels of FDI (see page 122)
  - rising productivity caused by foreign companies setting up in the UK and bringing with them new methods and ideas.

- London has become the world financial centre for the European time zone, bringing employment as well as large inflows of money.

- Globalisation has helped UK companies sell overseas – for many, 'Britishness' is part of the appeal.

- The UK is second only to the USA in the international provision of higher and further education.

- English is the language of the internet and of international business and commerce, giving the UK an advantage in developing e-commerce businesses and services.

- A wide range of products and goods are made available to UK consumers at low prices.

- There is a reduction in shortages of skilled labour due to international labour migration.

ACTIVITIES

In groups, see if you can come up with any other benefits. You could look at the government document Ensuring the UK benefits from globalisation (www.berr.gov.uk/files/file23447.pdf).

What are the costs of globalisation to the UK?

- Loss of jobs and manufacturing industry due to high costs, including wages. This has led to imports being cheaper, but also to UK firms moving production abroad.

- FDI may not prevent firms later moving to lower-cost countries, or returning home, if demand falls. This happened with both Siemens and Samsung in north-east England.

- The current account of the balance of payments has therefore shown a larger deficit.

- The UK is open to risks outside the control of the government – international capital flows and crises.

- Environmental problems are caused by the growth of air and sea transport, for goods but also for services such as tourism; by greater pollution in many low-cost countries increasing global warming; and by increased packaging leading to more waste.

- It will be harder for smaller businesses to establish themselves due to increased competition.

ACTIVITIES

In groups, see if you can come up with any other costs of globalisation.

FOR DEBATE

Divide the class into two groups. One group should prepare a presentation on the advantages, and the other on the disadvantages, of globalisation for the UK. If possible, present your arguments to a group of students who are *not* studying economics.

TAKING IT FURTHER

Make sure you have a good list of advantages and disadvantages, and that you understand the arguments on both sides.

Now write an answer of about 16 lines **evaluating** the extent to which globalisation has benefited the UK.

12 Why do some less developed countries struggle to achieve growth and benefit from international trade?

12.1 Poverty

UK businesses face competition both at home (from imports) and abroad.

APPLY IT!

40 years ago, an income of £1000 a year was seen as being good enough for a reasonable standard of living. It certainly provided enough to get a mortgage, and to feed, clothe and enjoy oneself. In 2009, many of you will live in a house where just the council tax is more than a £1000 – you would not be able to live on £1000 per year, you would be in poverty.

Try to calculate how much your family would need to spend just to survive – with no luxuries or non-essentials.

The World Bank says:

'Poverty is hunger. Poverty is lack of shelter. Poverty is being sick and not being able to see a doctor. Poverty is not having access to school and not knowing how to read. Poverty is not having a job, is fear for the future, living one day at a time. Poverty is losing a child to illness brought about by unclean water. Poverty is powerlessness, lack of representation and freedom.'

(Source: www.worldbank.org)

FOR DEBATE

Discuss whether you agree with the World Bank's statement. Has anything been left out, or should certain statements be omitted?

What is meant by absolute and relative poverty?

Absolute poverty is where someone has insufficient income to live on. It can be measured by adding up the cost of basic essentials such as food, clothing and shelter/housing. The amount of money needed to remain out of absolute poverty changes over time, and is different between countries.

KEY TERM

Absolute poverty – on a world basis is defined as having less than $1.25 a day to live on.

In eighteenth-century England, £100 a year was seen as a good income. In 2009, a day out for the family can easily cost £100.

Since 2008 the World Bank has defined absolute poverty in developing countries as having less than a $1.25 a day to live on. That is equivalent to about £325 a year.

In developed countries, very few people are in absolute poverty as the state intervenes to provide at least the bare necessities.

TAKING IT FURTHER

Go back to the World Bank's statement. How much of this is true for even the very poorest in the UK?

Relative poverty is more difficult to define. We are all relatively poor if we compare ourselves with Premier League footballers or film stars. We need to find a measure that allows us to determine those who are not in absolute poverty, but can't enjoy what many people see as essential.

The measure used by both the UK government and the EU as a target for relative poverty is 60% of median income. As shown by the map below, which shows percentage poverty rates in Europe at the 60% of average income margin, the UK has one of the higher rates of poverty in Europe.

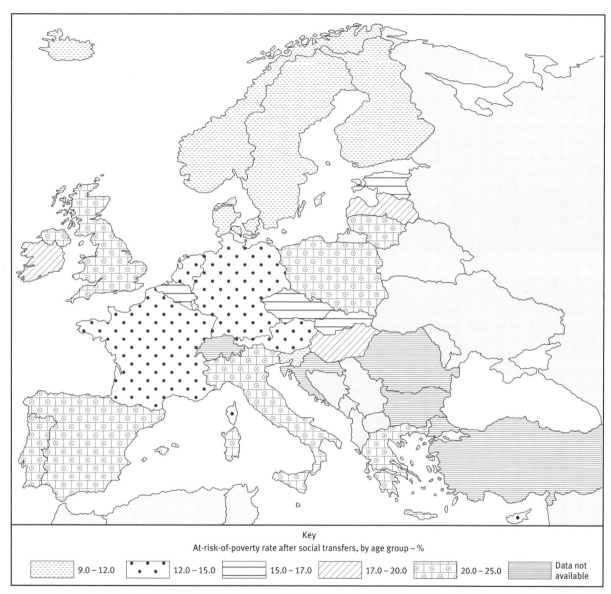

Key
At-risk-of-poverty rate after social transfers, by age group – %

9.0 – 12.0 · 12.0 – 15.0 · 15.0 – 17.0 · 17.0 – 20.0 · 20.0 – 25.0 · Data not available

(Source: eurostat website, http://epp.eurostat.ec.europa.eu)

Professor Townsend, a leading authority on poverty, defines poverty as when someone's 'resources are so seriously below those commanded by the average individual or family that they are, in effect, excluded from ordinary living patterns, customs and activities'. This definition depends on the society in which the person lives – it is relative.

 **ACTIVITIES**

AO1 and AO2 skills

Use www.poverty.org.uk to find out what is happening about poverty in the UK. Which groups are most at risk? Which groups have seen the greatest change in percentage in poverty? Why do you think this is the case? Discuss this in groups and give a short presentation of your ideas to the rest of the class.

How effective are policies aimed at reducing poverty?

In the UK, the government has concentrated on policies such as the National Minimum Wage and on a range of benefits such as Child Benefit and the State Pension.

FOR DEBATE

Compare the relative poverty of the *Big Issue* seller in UK with that of the bread seller in Morocco.

The graph shows the number of people on low incomes between 1979 and 2006. Although relative poverty has declined since the mid-1990s, it is still above the levels of the early 1980s. The main success over the past decade or so has been in reducing the number of pensioners and children in poverty. But it has proved more difficult to reduce the poverty levels of groups such as the disabled.

ACTIVITIES

AO1 and AO2 skills

Use the internet to find out more about what has happened to poverty in the UK as a result of specific policy changes.

In developing countries, absolute poverty has declined by over 20%, but excluding China, the fall is under 10%. The problem is that, in many of these countries, large groups are socially excluded. In these cases poverty is perpetuated through inequalities of power:

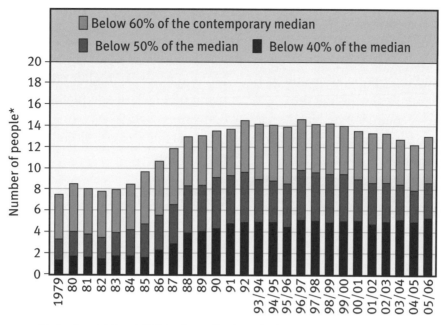

Below 60% of the contemporary median

Below 50% of the median   Below 40% of the median

*Number of people in households below the stated low income thresholds after deducting housing costs (millions)

The 50% median is the mid-point of all incomes.
(Source: The Poverty Site, Joseph Rowntree Foundation: www.poverty.org.uk)

- political – where the better-off tend to dominate positions of power and set agendas
- economic – for example, between bonded labourers and their employers/creditors
- social and cultural practices – from local-level exclusion of some individuals (such as widows or migrants) from village support networks, to widespread stereotyping of the poor, or of particular groups, as 'lazy' or 'backward' or 'unclean'.

Although the UK government claims it gives aid to countries to assist in reducing social exclusion, the Select Committee on Public Accounts, in its *Twenty-Seventh Report*, has cast doubt on its effectiveness.

TAKING IT FURTHER

Use the internet to find out more about world poverty and how it differs from country to country. Which groups are most affected?

FOR DEBATE

Discuss how effective policies have been in reducing poverty in different countries. Different groups could focus on different regions, for example a European country, China, an African country, etc. The findings could then be presented to allow a general conclusion to be drawn.

12.2 Limits to benefiting from globalisation

Developing countries and their populations often face problems when it comes to accessing the benefits of globalisation. A country may lack sufficient infrastructure or investment, or may suffer from a corrupt and/or inefficient government.

APPLY IT!

Rajesh lives in a small village in India. It has no electricity and is connected to the outside world by a dirt track road, which is often impassable when the rains come. He attends the village school, but knows that he will be expected to leave as soon as possible to help his father on their land. He would have loved to have gone to the school in the big city, but he has no idea how he could do so. He has heard of the big new buildings, schools where every student has a computer, shops with goods he can only imagine, and many well paid jobs. He can only dream of these.

Try to find out what village life is like in a developing country.

How does poor education and training limit the benefits of globalisation?

Education and training are vital in a world that depends more and more on advanced technology and knowledge. The competitiveness of countries is increasingly determined by their access to, and use of, knowledge.

The table below shows access to higher education.

Percentage of those aged 25–34 who have reached higher education (2006)	
Developed countries	30–60
Developing countries	10–20
Sub-Saharan African countries	5

Limited access to higher education is often a result of a lack of adequate primary and secondary education. UNESCO claims that 'in today's world, one in six adults is still not literate (two-thirds of them women)'.

FOR DEBATE

Discuss how a lack of education and training could affect the lives of people and the economy.

Which factors are important in limiting the benefits from globalisation?

While education and training are important factors, they are not the only ones. Some countries have poor healthcare, resulting in lower life expectancy and high infant mortality. In other cases, there is a lack of investment and foreign debts are large. In addition, civil wars and corruption have prevented people from benefiting from globalisation. The table on page 131 compares a range of factors in two African countries, India and the UK.

AO1 and AO2 skills ACTIVITIES

Investigate the factors shown in the table, and others, across a wider range of developing countries. Look at other countries in Africa, as well as some in Asia and South America. Use the information you gather in the following debate.

FOR DEBATE

Divide the class into four groups to consider:

- infrastructure, such as transport links
- health facilities
- population issues
- inward investment.

Each group should try to identify and discuss how problems linked to their topic could limit the benefits of globalisation.

	Chad	India	Kenya	UK
GDP				
Purchasing power parity (PPP) ($)	16.26 billion	3.267 trillion	61.83 billion	2231 trillion
Per capita ($)	1600	2800	1600	36 600
Infrastructure				
Paved roads: (km)	267	3 316 452	8933	398 366
Railways (km)	0	63 221	2778	16 567
Airports with paved runways	7	250	15	310
Education				
Literacy – % age ≥15 who can read and write	26	61	85	99
School/college life expectancy (years)	6	10	10	16
Education expenditure (% GDP)	1.9	3.2	6.9	5.6
Health				
Life expectancy (years)	48	70	58	79
HIV/AIDS – adult prevalence rate (%)	3.5	0.3	6.7	0.1
Foreign currency reserves ($)	1.12 billion	250 billion	3.12 billion	57.3 billion
Stock of FDI ($)	4.5 billion	142.9 billion	2.54 billion	1.41 trillion
Government	Ruled by an ethnic minority; suffers from civil war which has broken out on a regular basis.	Has had democratic rule since independence, but despite impressive gains in economic investment and output, faces pressing problems such as significant overpopulation, environmental degradation, extensive poverty, and widespread corruption.	For much of its independence, politics have been divided along tribal lines. Elections in 2007 brought charges of vote-rigging from the opposition and led to two months of violence in which 1500 people died. UN-sponsored talks led to a power-sharing government.	A stable democracy that has devolved some powers to assemblies in Northern Ireland, Scotland and Wales. A member of the European Union.
(Source: adapted from: CIA World Factbook: https://www.cia.gov)				

UK businesses face competition both at home (from imports) and abroad.

APPLY IT!

Ruth picked up her cup of coffee. On it was the statement: 'Your hot drink has been prepared using FAIRTRADE certified ingredients. You can enjoy this hot drink knowing that farmers and workers in developing countries receive a fair deal so that they can improve their lives.' She wondered to what extent they did benefit, and whether this was an effective way to support the growth of those economies.

Try to find out more about fair trade schemes in general, and any that operate in your town or area. How do they benefit growers? Does this lead to economic growth? How effective do you think they are?

Is aid better than trade?

Aid can be given both in terms of money, and in the form of goods (such as machinery, or people with specialist skills). Money can be given as a grant, or as a loan. But it was found that loans just led many countries into debt, which they couldn't pay back. In some cases, for every £1 received in aid, countries were paying back £2 in interest and repayments, thus making them poorer. In other situations, money was used by the country for prestige projects that provided little or no benefit to the people. So the UK government prefers to give grants for specific purposes.

APPLY IT!

For years, Bholaram Bhil has made a living from his patch of land in a village in Rajasthan, north-west India. But with water leakage from the field causing relatively low crop yields, Bholaram has found it increasingly difficult to support his family.

The UK-based charity Tearfund, which is currently receiving DFID funding, provided Bholaram with the knowledge to build a protective wall to keep rainwater inside his field.

Research other, similar projects funded by UK-based charities. Tearfund provided knowledge, not just the wall – why is that important?

Because of the problems with aid, and the fact that it targets only small, specific groups rather than the country as a whole, many believe that trade is better than aid. Developing countries benefit if they can trade with others that either are growing faster or are wealthier. The focus of the WTO, and its predecessor the GATT, was originally on removing trade barriers and placed heavy emphasis on the benefits of trade: 'Poor countries need to grow their way out of poverty and trade can serve as a key engine of that growth.'

More recently, there has been an emphasis on Aid for Trade – bringing the two together. Trade is seen as very important, but insufficient. This is because poor countries are not free to compete in the world's markets as they lack the advantages of rich countries. Without sound financial and legal systems, skilled, healthy workers and good infrastructure, they are unable to take advantage of trade opportunities. Only aid can provide these needs.

AO1 and AO2 skills ACTIVITIES

Use the Department for International Development website (www.dfid.gov.uk) to find out about the UK's policy on aid, and to which countries/projects this aid is given. Use www.wto.org to find out how trade has helped countries to grow.

How effective is investment?

Developing countries can be helped by investment in two ways.

Investment in a country's resources

Here we are going to consider just one aspect of this – investment in human capital. This is very important, as many developing countries do not invest enough in human capital. Formal schooling and vocational education and training are essential to equip people in those countries with the knowledge and skills that will allow them to benefit from training opportunities provided in the labour market, and will also attract foreign direct investment (FDI).

> **KEY TERM**
> **Foreign direct investment** – investment in productive assets by a company from another country.

Foreign direct investment

As demonstrated in the table below, FDI has become increasingly important in developing countries.

FDI inflows as a percentage of gross fixed capital (%)		
Region	**1986–91**	**1992–96**
Developed countries	3.5	3.2
Developing countries	3.4	6.8
Africa	3.9	7.2
Asia	2.8	6.0
Latin America	5.3	9.5
Central and Eastern Europe	0.1	6.2
(Source: www.unctad.org)		

FDI has very often meant accepting multinational corporations setting up in a country. The benefits of this have been very mixed. In some cases, although FDI increases, total investment falls as countries become over-reliant on inflows of capital.

FOR DEBATE

Why might over-reliance on FDI be a poor policy for a developing country?

How effective are debt relief programmes?

The foreign debt of many developing countries has hindered progress. In the 1990s, 41 countries, mostly in Africa, had total debt of $200 billion; their people (600 million) live about seven years less than citizens of other developing countries, and half live on less than $1 per day. Interest payments and debt repayments used up more than half their export earnings, thus limiting economic and social development. Since the mid-1990s, 23 countries have had their debts cancelled and a further 11 are being helped to achieve debt cancellation. This has enabled the money to be used for sustainable development and to relieve poverty.

AO1 and AO2 skills ACTIVITIES

Using the internet, try to find out more about debt relief. You may find the websites of the International Monetary Fund, the World Bank and the Department for International Development useful. Is it always a good idea to cancel developing countries' debts?

How effective are NGOs?

Non-government organisations (NGOs) are bodies such as Oxfam and Save the Children. They are often charities which have specific purposes, and are thus very focused on particular problems.

TAKING IT FURTHER

Select an NGO of your choice. Using the internet, research what it is doing to help developing countries. Prepare a five-minute presentation explaining what it does and how effective you think it is.

ExamCafé

Welcome to the Exam Café for Part 3

Revision

REVISION TIP

Revision is boring – don't fall into the trap of just reading your notes over and over again and sending yourself to sleep!

REVISION TIP

Make revision ACTIVE:

- read those notes in small chunks, one or two chapters at a time
- test yourself – ask a friend, or even a parent/grandparent or younger brother/sister, to test your knowledge of key concepts, making a game of it or having a prize for meeting a target – it must be a challenge
- try doing questions – do some against the clock (don't cheat!) and others in the form of notes/spider diagrams, etc.
- keep up-to-date – read a newspaper; look at websites such as http://news.bbc.co.uk and click on 'business' and its subsections
- have fun – look at a website such as www.bized.co.uk and click on 'learning materials' to find extra ideas for economics, and on 'virtual worlds' for a chance to try out your understanding.

Common mistakes

Do not confuse the following.
- The **balance of payments** with the **budget** (see ExamCafe for Unit 2).
- The **value** of the pound – that is, the exchange rate – with the **purchasing power** of the pound in the UK. A fall in the value of the pound does not mean we can buy fewer goods in the UK.
- The **direction in which goods and services move** with **what happens to money paid** for them. This is very easy to do with imports of services – for example, if we go on holiday to France, that is an import because we pay money to the French hotel/campsite we stay in.
- The **EU** with the **eurozone** – the UK is a member of the EU, but not of the euro.
- **Absolute poverty** and **relative poverty**.

REVISION TIP

To maximise your chances of success:

- revise thoroughly
- discover sources of discussion/comment and analysis – not more knowledge
- practise past questions under timed conditions
- practise evaluation
- don't remember the answers, but the *principles* – you aren't going to answer last year's paper
- seek out different ways in which international economics data are presented – are you familiar with data on different topics?
- RTQ! (see page 137)

REVISION CHECKLIST – Part 3

● Not confident
● Needs more revision
○ Confident

	●	●	○
Why do countries trade?			
Globalisation			
Explain what is meant by globalisation.			
Evaluate the factors that have contributed to the growth of globalisation, including the impact of new technology.			
Give examples of, and explain what is meant by, a multinational company.			
Evaluate the role of multinational companies in globalisation.			
International specialisation and trade			
Understand the meaning of specialisation.			
Understand and apply the principles of absolute advantage (calculations of absolute advantage are not required).			
Appreciate the advantages of trade and the consequences of global interdependence.			
Explain the possible negative externalities associated with trade, e.g. increased pollution.			

	Not confident ●	Needs more revision ●	Confident ○	●	●	○
World Trade Organization						
Explain what is meant by free trade.						
Evaluate the arguments for free trade.						
Understand the role of the World Trade Organization in promoting free trade.						
Patterns of trade						
Explain what is meant by an import and an export.						
Identify the UK's main imports and exports with the EU and the rest of the world.						
Evaluate the impact of changes in trading patterns on the UK and the EU.						
Evaluate the potential impact of China and India on patterns of world trade.						
Protectionism						
Understand the reasons for protection.						
Identify the methods of protection, such as tariffs and quotas.						
Evaluate the methods of protection.						
Why is the UK in the European Union?						
Membership of the EU						
Identify the member countries of the EU and the eurozone.						
Explain and evaluate the advantages and disadvantages of the single market.						
Explain and evaluate the advantages and disadvantages of the single currency.						
How is the UK's international trade recorded?						
Balance of payments						
Identify the components of the current account.						
Calculate the balance of trade in goods, the balance of trade in services and the current account balance.						
Balance of payments deficit						
Explain what is meant by a balance of payments deficit and surplus.						
Understand the reasons for a balance of payments deficit.						
Evaluate the methods of rectifying a balance of payments deficit.						
How important is the value of a currency?						
Exchange rates						
Explain what is meant by an exchange rate.						
Understand and illustrate how exchange rates are determined through the interaction of demand and supply.						
Understand how exchange rates may be influenced by interest rates.						
Explain and evaluate the impact of changes in exchange rates on trade and international competitiveness.						
How does a country become more competitive?						
Factors influencing competitiveness						
Appreciate the importance of wages and relative unit labour costs.						
Understand the importance of the exchange rate.						
Understand the importance of productivity.						
Understand the importance of other costs.						
Government policy and international competitiveness						
Understand the importance of low inflation.						
Understand the importance of sustainable economic growth.						
Understand the importance of incentives for investment.						
Evaluate the importance of investment in education and training.						
Discuss and evaluate government policies aimed at improving UK international competitiveness.						
The UK and globalisation						
Evaluate the extent to which globalisation has benefited the UK.						
Why do some less developed countries struggle to achieve growth and benefit from international trade?						
Poverty						
Explain the difference between absolute and relative poverty.						
Explain absolute poverty and relative poverty.						
Discuss and evaluate the impact of policies aimed at reducing poverty.						

continued

Exam**Café**

● Not confident ● Needs more revision ○ Confident	●	●	○
Limits to benefiting from globalisation			
Evaluate such factors as poor infrastructure, poor education and training, health and population problems, debt, weak government and corruption, low inward investment, lack of foreign currency, etc.			
What measures may be used to support growth for less developed countries?			
Ways of supporting growth			
Evaluate factors such as:			
• aid			
• trade			
• debt relief			
• investment			
• help with investment in human capital			
• fair trade schemes			
• non-government organisations.			

REVISION MATRIX

Copy out and complete this revision matrix.

Question	Globalisation	Single market	Current account of the balance of payments	Exchange rate
How is it defined?				
How does it affect the UK economy?				

Exam Preparation

This will be a paper-based exam and will be 1.5 hours in length. Candidates are required to answer a series of questions based on pre-released stimulus material. Some of the questions may involve data interpretation. All questions in this paper will be compulsory. This exam will be worth 50% of your total GCSE Economics mark.

EXAM TIPS

Read The Question – RTQ!

There are three major reasons why people underperform in exams, other than they haven't bothered to revise.

1. They fail to read the question and any data/material that goes with it.
   - Allocate some time to read through all the extracts – they are all there for a purpose. About 10 minutes could be given for this.
   - All the words in a question are there for a purpose – don't ignore them.
   - Don't pick on one or two terms you know and ignore the rest – this will drastically cut the marks you can get.

2. They don't address the command words – such as 'explain' or 'discuss'.
   - These words tell you what to do.
   - Failure to notice them will severely limit the marks you can get.

3. They ignore the number of marks for the question.
   - These tell you how much to write – ignore them, and you will write too much (a waste of time) or too little (reducing your chance of gaining full marks).
   - They tell you how long to spend on each question.
   - For Unit 3 you have 90 minutes for 80 marks – roughly 1 mark = 1 minute, so for a two-mark question don't spend more than 2 minutes.

Understanding exam language

State, Name, Identify, Which – all signify answers that require only a few words (in many cases, only one word), or one or more figures. There is no need to write complete sentences.

Describe – is an extended version of state, etc., and *does* require a sentence.

Compare – means to bring out the differences and similarities between two years, countries, etc. Do not write out the data.

Explain – it is vital to look and see both the number of marks given, and how many points are required. It requires you to state some knowledge and then to develop it. If there are 4 marks, then some analysis (use of economic language/terms/concepts) is being looked for in the answer.

Discuss, Do you agree, To what extent, Recommend, Give reasons for your answer, Evaluate – these all require a supported answer, usually asking you to explain at least two points or two different positions (e.g. free trade and protection), and then coming to a conclusion drawn from what you have written.

Look back at the advice given in ExamCafe at the end of Unit 2 under 'Understanding Exam Language' for more information on what these words mean.

IN THE EXAM ROOM

- Read *all* the information before starting a question.
- Make sure you identify the command word and respond to it – especially 'discuss', etc.
- Manage your time carefully.
- Write clear English and try to spell correctly. The examiner can only mark what you have written, not what you meant to write.
- Remember to label diagrams fully.
- If you finish early, read through what you have written to check it makes sense.
- RTQ!

Exam**Café**

Sample questions

(a) Using the chart, describe what has happened to the UK's balance of trade between January 2008 and March 2009.
(2 marks)

UK balance of trade in goods and services, January 2008 to March 2009

(*Source*: www.statistics.gov.uk/cci/nugget.asp?ID=199)

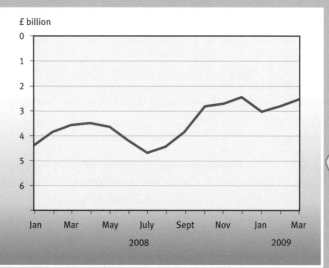

£ billion

Raj's answer

It has gone up from −£4.2bn to −£2.5bn.

Ewawa's answer

It has improved with some fluctuations from −£4.2bn to −£2.5bn.

Examiner says: Both candidates have correctly identified the figures and that they are negative (1 mark). But 'it has gone up' is meaningless, especially when the figures are negative, whereas Ewawa has made the important point that there has been an overall improvement (1 mark).

(b) Explain two reasons why the UK has a negative balance of trade. *(4 marks)*

Raj's answer

Reason: fall in manufacturing.

Explain: we import more from China

Reason: membership of the EU

Explain: this means that we have to let in EU goods without tariffs so our firms close

Ewawa's answer

Reason: decline in manufacturing industry.

Explain: many UK firms have moved their manufacturing to low cost countries such as Thailand.

Reason: high value of the £.

Explain: this has meant that UK goods are less competitive while imports are cheaper leading to less exports and more imports.

Examiner says: Both candidates have correctly identified a fall in manufacturing in the UK (1 mark), but Raj's explanation does not really explain the reason (it is half true, but with only 1 mark available it scores zero), unlike Ewawa's, which is a clear explanation and shows understanding gained in the course. For the second reason, Ewawa chose another good economic factor which affected UK trade in the mid-2000s and then offers a full explanation. Raj has allowed prejudice to replace economics. While we may import more from the EU, these goods replace those from other countries. Ewawa scored 4 marks, but Raj only 1 mark.

(c) Discuss how the UK government could try to improve the balance of trade.
(8 marks)

Raj's answer

The UK could impose tariff barriers to make imports more expensive and thus help UK firms. It could also impose quotas to limit imports or could even ban some goods so we bought British ones. We could also leave the EU. All of these would mean an improvement in the balance of trade.

Examiner says: Raj has shown some knowledge from the course and offered some explanation, but it is limited and there is no discussion. This was awarded 3 marks.

Ewawa's answer

In theory we could impose trade barriers, but these would be against both our membership of the EU and the WTO and would lead to more problems. These are not therefore measures open to the UK.

It would be better for the UK to improve its competitiveness. This could be done through better education and training so that people have the skills needed for working today and in the future. We could also encourage firms to invest more in research and development and in new capital equipment. This could increase productivity and reduce costs as well as leading to new products.

I think that education and training is the best way, although it takes time, because this would achieve the same outcome as investment, but also ensure that we were equipped to deal with changes to come.

Ewawa's is an excellent answer that recognises the actual situation the UK is in offering a brief evaluation and then explains two valid ideas before going on to provide a supported conclusion. 8 marks.

To what extent has globalisation helped to reduce world poverty? Give reasons for your answer.

Frances's answer

Globalisation has helped to increase world trade. For many African countries this had meant more exports and thus a rise in employment and incomes reducing poverty. Equally, globalisation has seen manufacturing move from high cost to low cost countries having a similar effect on their people. This has also spread the benefits of technology so that poorer countries can gain knowledge to help them develop further. All of this shows that globalisation has had a considerable effect on reducing poverty.

Examiner says: the case for globalisation is clearly explained.

The recent recession has shown, however, that the benefits can rapidly disappear with millions becoming unemployed in China and possibly returning to poverty. Multinational companies may create jobs, but most of the profits are sent back to the rich countries so that any gain is very limited. There is also nothing stopping them from packing up and moving elsewhere. Evidence from India shows that although many have gained from new jobs, for those in poverty there have been few if any benefits.

Examiner says: the case against globalisation is clearly explained.

It is difficult to decide the extent to which globalisation has reduced poverty. Even though there are reservations about the effects, there is some good evidence to show that overall the benefits have outweighed any disadvantages. It is clear though that there are a range of factors which need to be put in place to supplement globalisation such as better education and healthcare. All one can say is that globalisation has had some effect on reducing poverty.

Examiner says: Frances has come to a supported conclusion based on what she wrote in the previous paragraphs. She has addressed the 'to what extent' element as well as giving reasons for her answer. Overall, Frances has made an excellent attempt at a difficult question. She is clearly aware of what is happening in the world economy.

Sample exam questions (Part 3)

1

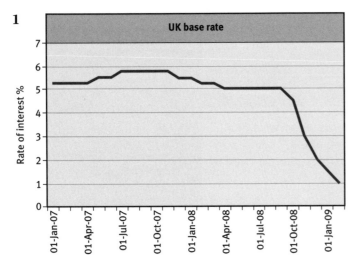

Figure 1

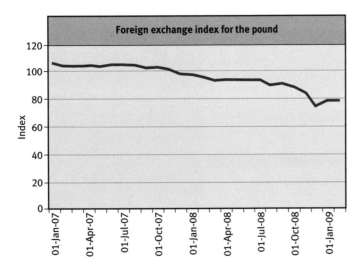

Figure 2

(a) Using Figure 1, state the value for the highest rate of interest in the period January 2007 to January 2009. (1)

(b) Using Figure 1, describe what has happened to the UK's rate of interest between September 2007 and January 2009. (2)

(c) (i) Using Figures 1 and 2, compare changes in the rate of interest and the exchange rate between November 2007 and January 2009. (2)

    (ii) Explain how changes in the rate of interest could affect the exchange rate. (4)

(d) How might the changes to the value of the pound shown in Figure 2 affect the UK's current account? Explain your answer. (4)

2

Crisis Jolts Globalization Process

Economic and financial globalization and the expansion of world trade have brought substantial benefits to countries around the world. But the current financial crisis has put globalization on hold, with capital flows reversing and global trade shrinking. The danger is that some countries may be tempted to introduce protectionist measures.

Source: www.imf.org/external/np/exr/key/global.htm

Japan saw unemployment levels reach a six-year high last month, with job availability at a new low, official figures have shown. The jobless number increased by 830,000 in June, or 31.3% from a year before, to 3.48 million.

Unemployment in Germany rose in July, official figures have shown, and economists have warned that the worst still lies ahead for the job market.

China's job outlook remains very grave and could deteriorate further. One-third of last year's university graduates, three million former students, have not yet found employment.

Source: http://news.bbc.co.uk/1/hi/business/8183144.stm

(a) (i) State two benefits that globalisation has brought to 'countries around the world'. (2)

    (ii) By how much has unemployment increased in Japan during the past year? (1)

(b) Explain how 'global trade shrinking' could lead to:

    (i) rising unemployment across the world. (2)

    (ii) increased poverty in developing countries. (2)

(c) (i) Name two protectionist measures that a country could impose on trade. (2)

    (ii) Explain why many people are worried that there could be an increase in trade protection. (4)

(d) In view of the current world recession, discuss whether globalisation is of benefit to developing countries. (6)

Answers and mark schemes are available online, go to www.heinemann.co.uk

Index